Charles King

Army Life on the Frontier (1890)

Charles King
Army Life on the Frontier (1890)
ISBN/EAN: 9783743422933
Manufactured in Europe, USA, Canada, Australia, Japa
Cover: Foto ©ninafisch / pixelio.de

Manufactured and distributed by brebook publishing software (www.brebook.com)

Charles King

Army Life on the Frontier (1890)

CAPT. CHARLES KING'S
POPULAR MILITARY NOVELS.

THE COLONEL'S DAUGHTER.
Illustrated. 12mo. Extra cloth. $1.25.

MARION'S FAITH.
Illustrated. 12mo. Extra cloth. $1.25.

STARLIGHT RANCH, and Other Stories.
12mo. Cloth. $1.00.

KITTY'S CONQUEST.
12mo. Extra cloth. $1.00.

LARAMIE; or, The Queen of Bedlam.
12mo. Cloth. $1.00.

THE DESERTER, and FROM THE RANKS.
12mo. Extra cloth. $1.00.

TWO SOLDIERS, and DUNRAVEN RANCH.
12mo. Extra cloth. $1.00.

"It is a relief, indeed, to turn from the dismal introspection of much of our modern fiction to the fresh naturalness of such stories as these."—*N. Y. Critic.*

"No military novels of the day rival those of Capt. King in precision and popularity."—*Boston Courier.*

J. B. LIPPINCOTT COMPANY, Publishers,
PHILADELPHIA.

STARLIGHT RANCH

AND

OTHER STORIES OF ARMY
LIFE ON THE FRONTIER.

BY

CAPTAIN CHARLES KING, U.S.A.,
AUTHOR OF
"MARION'S FAITH," "THE COLONEL'S DAUGHTER," ETC.

PHILADELPHIA:
J. B. LIPPINCOTT COMPANY.
1891.

CONTENTS.

	PAGE
STARLIGHT RANCH	7
WELL WON; OR, FROM THE PLAINS TO "THE POINT"	40
FROM "THE POINT" TO THE PLAINS	116
THE WORST MAN IN THE TROOP	201
VAN	234

STARLIGHT RANCH.

WE were crouching round the bivouac fire, for the night was chill, and we were yet high up along the summit of the great range. We had been scouting through the mountains for ten days, steadily working southward, and, though far from our own station, our supplies were abundant, and it was our leader's purpose to make a clean sweep of the line from old Sandy to the Salado, and fully settle the question as to whether the renegade Apaches had betaken themselves, as was possible, to the heights of the Matitzal, or had made a break for their old haunts in the Tonto Basin or along the foot-hills of the Black Mesa to the east. Strong scouting-parties had gone thitherward, too, for "the Chief" was bound to bring these Tontos to terms; but our orders were explicit: "Thoroughly scout the east face of the Matitzal." We had capital Indian allies with us. Their eyes were keen, their legs tireless, and there had been bad blood between them and the tribe now broken away from the reservation. They asked nothing better than a chance to shoot and kill them; so we could feel well assured that if "Tonto sign" appeared anywhere along our path it would instantly be reported. But now we were south of the confluence of Tonto Creek and the Wild Rye, and our scouts declared that beyond that point was the territory of the White Mountain Apaches, where we would not be likely to find the renegades.

East of us, as we lay there in the sheltered nook whence the glare of our fire could not be seen, lay the deep valley of the Tonto brawling along its rocky bed on the way to join the Salado, a few short marches farther south. Beyond it, though we could not see them now, the peaks and "buttes" of the Sierra Ancha rolled up as massive foot-hills to the Mogollon. All through there our scouting-parties had hitherto been able to find Indians whenever they really wanted to. There were some officers who couldn't find the Creek itself if they thought Apaches lurked along its bank, and of such, some of us thought, was our leader.

In the dim twilight only a while before I had heard our chief packer exchanging confidences with one of the sergeants,—

"I tell you, Harry, if the old man were trying to steer clear of all possibility of finding these Tontos, he couldn't have followed a better track than ours has been. And he made it, too; did you notice? Every time the scouts tried to work out to the left he would herd them all back—up-hill."

"We never did think the lieutenant had any too much sand," answered the sergeant, grimly; "but any man with half an eye can see that orders to thoroughly scout the east face of a range does not mean keep on top of it as we've been doing. Why, in two more marches we'll be beyond their stamping-ground entirely, and then it's only a slide down the west face to bring us to those ranches in the Sandy Valley. Ever seen them?"

"No. I've never been this far down; but what do you want to bet that *that's* what the lieutenant is aiming at? He wants to get a look at that pretty girl all the fellows at Fort Phœnix are talking about."

"Dam'd old gray-haired rip! It would be just like him. With a wife and kids up at Sandy too."

There were officers in the party, junior in years of life and years of service to the gray-headed subaltern whom some odd fate had assigned to the command of this detachment, nearly two complete "troops" of cavalry with a pack-train of sturdy little mules to match. We all knew that, as organized, one of our favorite captains had been assigned the command, and that between "the Chief," as we called our general, and him a perfect understanding existed as to just how thorough and searching this scout should be. The general himself came down to Sandy to superintend the start of the various commands, and rode away after a long interview with our good old colonel, and after seeing the two parties destined for the Black Mesa and the Tonto Basin well on their way. We were to move at nightfall the following day, and within an hour of the time of starting a courier rode in from Prescott with despatches (it was before our military telegraph line was built), and the commander of the division—the superior of our Arizona chief—ordered Captain Tanner to repair at once to San Francisco as witness before an important court-martial. A groan went up from more than one of us when we heard the news, for it meant nothing less than that the command of the most important expedition of all would now devolve upon the senior first lieutenant, Gleason; and so much did it worry Mr. Blake, his junior by several files, that he went at once to Colonel Pelham, and begged to be relieved from duty with that column and ordered to overtake one of the others. The colonel, of course, would listen to nothing of the kind, and to Gleason's immense and evident gratification we were marched forth under his command. There had been no friction, however. Despite his gray beard, Gleason was not an old man, and he really strove to be courteous and conciliatory to his officers,—he was always considerate towards his men; but by the time we had been out ten days, having accomplished nothing, most of us were thoroughly disgusted. Some few ventured to remonstrate. Angry words passed between the commander and Mr. Blake, and on the night on which our story begins there was throughout the command a feeling that we were simply being trifled with.

The chat between our chief packer and Sergeant Merrick ceased instantly as I came forward and passed them on the way to look over the herd guard of the little battalion, but it set me to thinking. This was not the first that the officers of the Sandy garrison had heard of those two new "ranches" established within the year down in the hot but fertile valley, and not more than four hours' easy gallop from Fort Phœnix, where a couple of troops of "Ours" were stationed. The people who had so confidently planted themselves there were evidently well to do, and they brought with them a good-sized retinue of ranch- and herdsmen,— mainly Mexicans,—plenty of "stock," and a complete "camp outfit," which served them well until they could raise the adobe walls and finish their homesteads.

Curiosity led occasional parties of officers or enlisted men to spend a day in saddle and thus to visit these enterprising neighbors. Such parties were always civilly received, invited to dismount, and soon to take a bite of luncheon with the proprietors, while their horses were promptly led away, unsaddled, rubbed down, and at the proper time fed and watered. The officers, of course, had introduced themselves and proffered the hospitality and assistance of the fort. The proprietors had expressed all proper appreciation, and declared that if anything should happen to be needed they would be sure to call; but they were too busy, they explained, to make social visits. They were hard at work, as the gentlemen could see, getting up their houses and their corrals, for, as one of them expressed it, "We've come to stay." There were three of these pioneers; two of them, brothers evidently, gave the name of Crocker. The third, a tall, swarthy, all-over-frontiersman, was introduced by the others as Mr. Burnham. Subsequent investigations led to the fact that Burnham was first cousin to the Crockers. "Been long in Arizona?" had been asked, and the elder Crocker promptly replied, "No, only a year,— mostly prospecting."

The Crockers were building down towards the stream; but Burnham, from some freak which he did not explain, had driven his stakes and was slowly getting up his walls half a mile south of the other homestead, and high up on a spur of foot-hill that stood at least three hundred feet above the general level of the valley. From his "coigne of vantage" the whitewashed walls and the bright colors of the flag of the fort could be dimly made out,—twenty odd miles down stream.

"Every now and then," said Captain Wayne, who happened up our way on a general court, "a bull-train —a small one—went past the fort on its way up to the ranches, carrying lumber and all manner of supplies, but they never stopped and camped near the post either going or coming, as other trains were sure to do. They never seemed to want anything, even at the sutler's store, though the Lord knows there wasn't much there they *could* want except tanglefoot and tobacco. The bull-train made perhaps six trips in as many months, and by that time the glasses at the fort could make out that Burnham's place was all finished, but never once had either of the three proprietors put in an appearance, as invited, which was considered not only extraordinary but unneighborly, and everybody quit riding out there."

"But the funniest thing," said Wayne, "happened one night when I was officer of the day. The road up-stream ran within a hundred yards of the post of the sentry on No. 3, which post was back of the officer's quarters, and a quarter of a mile above the stables, corrals, etc. I was making the rounds about one o'clock in the morning. The night was bright and clear, though the moon was low, and I came upon Dexter, one of the sharpest men in my troop, as the sentry on No. 3. After I had given him the countersign and was about going on,—for there was no use in asking *him* if he knew his orders,—he stopped me to ask if I had authorized the stable-sergeant to let out one of the ambulances within the hour.

Of course I was amazed and said no. 'Well,' said he, 'not ten minutes ago a four-mule ambulance drove up the road yonder going full tilt, and I thought something was wrong, but it was far beyond my challenge limit.' You can understand that I went to the stables on the jump, ready to scalp the sentry there, the sergeant of the guard, and everybody else. I sailed into the sentry first and he was utterly astonished; he swore that every horse, mule, and wagon was in its proper place. I routed out the old stable-sergeant and we went through everything with his lantern. There wasn't a spoke or a hoof missing. Then I went back to Dexter and asked him what he'd been drinking, and he seemed much hurt. I told him every wheel at the fort was in its proper rut and that nothing could have gone out. Neither could there have been a four-mule ambulance from elsewhere. There wasn't a civilized corral within fifty miles except those new ranches up the valley, and *they* had no such rig. All the same, Dexter stuck to his story, and it ended in our getting a lantern and going down to the road. By Gad! he was right. There, in the moist, yielding sand, were the fresh tracks of a four-mule team and a Concord wagon or something of the same sort. So much for *that* night!

"Next evening as a lot of us were sitting out on the major's piazza, and young Briggs of the infantry was holding forth on the constellations,—you know he's a good deal of an astronomer,—Mrs. Powell suddenly turned to him with 'But you haven't told us the name of that bright planet low down there in the northern sky,' and we all turned and looked where she pointed.

Briggs looked too. It was only a little lower than some stars of the second and third magnitude that he had been telling about only five minutes before, only it shone with a redder or yellower glare,—orange I suppose was the real color,—and was clear and strong as the light of Jupiter.

"'That?' says Briggs. 'Why, that must be—— Well, I own up. I declare I never knew there was so big a star in that part of the firmament!'

"'Don't worry about it, Briggs, old boy,' drawled the major, who had been squinting at it through a powerful glass he owns. 'That's terra firmament. That planet's at the new ranch up on the spur of the Matitzal.'

"But that wasn't all. Two days after, Baker came in from a scout. He had been over across the range and had stopped at Burnham's on his way down. He didn't see Burnham; he wasn't invited in, but he was full of his subject. 'By *Jove!* fellows. Have any of you been to the ranches lately? No? Well, then, I want to get some of the ladies to go up there and call. In all my life I never saw so pretty a girl as was sitting there on the piazza when I rode around the corner of the house. *Pretty!* She's lovely. Not Mexican. No, indeed! A real American girl,—a young lady, by Gad!" That, then, explained the new light.

"And did that give the ranch the name by which it is known to you?" we asked Wayne.

"Yes. The ladies called it 'Starlight Ranch' from that night on. But not one of them has seen the girl. Mrs. Frazer and Mrs. Jennings actually took the long drive and asked for the ladies, and were civilly told that there were none at home. It was a Chinese servant who received them. They inquired for Mr. Burnham and he was away too. They asked how many ladies there were, and the Chinaman shook his head—'No sabe.' 'Had Mr. Burnham's wife and daughter come?' 'No sabe.' 'Were Mr. Burnham and the ladies over at the other ranch?' 'No sabe,' still affably grinning, and evidently personally pleased to see the strange ladies; but that Chinaman was no fool; he had his instructions and was carrying them out; and Mrs. Frazer, whose eyes are very keen, was confident that she saw the curtains in an upper window gathered just so as to admit a pair of eyes to peep down at the fort wagon with its fair occupants. But the face of which she caught a glimpse was not that of a young woman. They gave the Chinaman their cards, which he curiously inspected and was evidently at a loss what to do with, and after telling him to give them to the ladies when they came home they drove over to the Crocker Ranch. Here only Mexicans were visible about the premises, and, though Mrs. Frazer's Spanish was equal to the task of asking them for water for herself and friend, she could not get an intelligible reply from the swarthy Ganymede who brought them the brimming glasses as to the ladies—*Las señoras*—at the other ranch. They asked for the Crockers, and the Mexican only vaguely pointed up the valley. It was in defeat and humiliation that the ladies with their escort, Mr. Baker, returned to the fort, but Baker rode up again and took a comrade with him, and they both saw the girl with the lovely face and form this time, and had almost accosted her when a sharp, stern voice called her within. A fortnight more and a dozen men, officers or soldiers, had rounded that ranch and had seen two women,—one middle-aged, the other a girl of about eighteen who was fair and bewitchingly pretty. Baker had bowed to her and she had smiled sweetly on him, even while being drawn within doors. One or two men had cornered Burnham and began to ask questions. 'Gentlemen,' said he, 'I'm a poor hand at talk. I've no education. I've lived on the frontier all my life. I mean no offence, but I cannot answer your questions and I cannot ask you into my house. For explanation, I refer you to Mr. Crocker.' Then Baker and a chum of his rode over and called on the elder Crocker, and asked for the explanation. That only added to the strangeness of the thing.

"'It is true, gentlemen, that Mr. Burnham's wife and child are now with him; but, partially because of her, his wife's, infirm health, and partially because of a most distressing and unfortunate experience in his past, our kinsman begs that no one will attempt to call at the ranch. He appreciates all the courtesy the gentlemen and ladies at the fort would show, and have shown, but he feels compelled to decline all intercourse. We are beholden, in a measure, to Mr. Burnham, and have to be guided by his wishes. We are young men compared to him, and it was through him that we came to seek our fortune here, but he is virtually the head of both establishments.' Well. There was nothing more to be said, and the boys came away. One thing more transpired. Burnham gave it out that he had lived in Texas before the war, and had fought all the way through in the Confederate service. He thought the officers ought to know this. It was the major himself to whom he told it, and when the major replied that he considered the war over and that that made no difference, Burnham, with a clouded face replied, 'Well, mebbe it don't—to you.' Whereupon the major fired up and told him that if he chose to be an unreconstructed reb, when Union officers and gentlemen were only striving to be civil to him, he might 'go ahead and be d—d,' and came away in high dudgeon." And so matters stood up to the last we had heard from Fort Phœnix, except for one letter which Mrs. Frazer wrote to Mrs. Turner at Sandy, perhaps purely out of feminine mischief, because a year or so previous Baker, as a junior second lieutenant, was doing the devoted to Mrs. Turner, a species of mildly amatory apprenticeship which most of the young officers seemed impelled to serve on first joining. "We are having such a romance here at Phœnix. You have doubtless heard of the beautiful girl at 'Starlight Ranch,' as we call the Burnham place, up the valley. Everybody who called has been rebuffed; but, after catching a few glimpses of her, Mr. Baker became completely infatuated and rode up that way three or four times a week. Of late he has ceased going in the daytime, but it is known that he rides out towards dusk and gets back long after midnight, sometimes not till morning. Of course it takes four hours, nearly, to come from there full-speed, but though Major Tracy will admit nothing, it must be that Mr. Baker has his permission to be away at night. We all believe that it is another case of love laughing at locksmiths and that in some way they contrive to meet. One thing is certain,—Mr. Baker is desperately in love and will permit no trifling with him on the subject." Ordinarily, I suppose, such a letter would have been gall and wormwood to Mrs. Turner, but as young Hunter, a new appointment, was now a devotee, and as it was a piece of romantic news which interested all Camp Sandy, she read the letter to one lady after another, and so it became public property. Old Catnip, as we called the colonel, was disposed to be a little worried on the subject. Baker was a youngster in whom he had some interest as being a distant connection of his wife's, but Mrs. Pelham had not come to Arizona with us, and the good old fellow was living *en garçon* with the Mess, where, of course, the matter was discussed in all its bearings.

All these things recurred to me as I pottered around through the herds examining side-lines, etc., and looking up the guards. Ordinarily our scouting parties were so small that we had no such thing as an officer-of-the-day,—nor had we now when Gleason could have been excused for ordering one, but he evidently desired to do nothing that might annoy his officers. He *might* want them to stand by him when it came to reporting the route and result of the scout. All the same, he expected that the troop officers would give personal supervision to their command, and especially to look after their "herds," and it was this duty that took me away from the group chatting about the bivouac fire preparatory to "turning in" for the night.

When I got back, a tall, gray-haired trooper was "standing attention" in front of the commanding officer, and had evidently just made some report, for Mr.

Gleason nodded his head appreciatively and then said, kindly,—

"You did perfectly right, corporal. Instruct your men to keep a lookout for it, and if seen again to-night to call me at once. I'll bring my field-glass and we'll see what it is."

The trooper raised his left hand to the "carried" carbine in salute and turned away. When he was out of earshot, Gleason spoke to the silent group,—

"Now, there's a case in point. If I had command of a troop and could get old Potts into it I could make something of him, and I know it."

Gleason had consummate faith in his "system" with the rank and file, and no respect for that of any of the captains. Nobody said anything. Blake hated him and puffed unconcernedly at his pipe, with a display of absolute indifference to his superior's views that the latter did not fail to note. The others knew what a trial "old Potts" had been to his troop commander, and did not believe that Gleason could "reform" him at will. The silence was embarrassing, so I inquired,—

"What had he to report?"

"Oh, nothing of any consequence. He and one of the sentries saw what they took to be an Indian signal-fire up Tonto Creek. It soon smouldered away,—but I always make it a point to show respect to these old soldiers."

"You show d——d little respect for their reports all the same," said Blake, suddenly shooting up on a pair of legs that looked like stilts. "An Indian signal-fire is a matter of a heap of consequence in my opinion;" and he wrathfully stalked away.

For some reason Gleason saw fit to take no notice of this piece of insubordination. Placidly he resumed his chat,—

"Now, you gentlemen seem skeptical about Potts. Do any of you know his history?"

"Well, I know he's about the oldest soldier in the regiment; that he served in the First Dragoons when they were in Arizona twenty years ago, and that he gets drunk as a boiled owl every pay-day," was an immediate answer.

"Very good as far as it goes," replied Gleason, with a superior smile; "but I'll just tell you a chapter in his life he never speaks of and I never dreamed of until the last time I was in San Francisco. There I met old General Starr at the 'Occidental,' and almost the first thing he did was to inquire for Potts, and then he told me about him. He was one of the finest sergeants in Starr's troop in '53,—a dashing, handsome fellow,—and while in at Fort Leavenworth he had fallen in love with, won, and married as pretty a young girl as ever came into the regiment. She came out to New Mexico with the detachment with which he served, and was the belle of all the '*bailes*' given either by the 'greasers' or the enlisted men. He was proud of her as he could be, and old Starr swore that the few ladies of the regiment who were with them at old Fort Fillmore or Stanton were really jealous of her. Even some of the young officers got to saying sweet things to her, and Potts came to the captain about it, and he had it stopped; but the girl's head was turned. There was a handsome young fellow in the sutler's store who kept making her presents on the sly, and when at last Potts found it out he nearly hammered the life out of him. Then came that campaign against the Jicarilla Apaches, and Potts had to go with his troop and leave her at the cantonment, where, to be sure, there were ladies and plenty of people to look after her; and in the fight at Cieneguilla poor Potts was badly wounded, and it was some months before they got back; and meantime the sutler fellow had got in his work, and when the command finally came in with its wounded they had skipped, no one knew where. If Potts hadn't been taken down with brain fever on top of his wound he would have followed their trail, desertion or no desertion, but he was a broken man when he got out of hospital. The last thing old Starr said to me was, 'Now, Gleason, I want you to be kind to my old sergeant; he served all through the war, and I've never forgiven them in the First for going back on him and refusing to re-enlist him; but the captains, one and all, said it was no use; he had sunk lower and lower; was perfectly unreliable; spent nine-tenths of his time in the guard-house and all his money in whiskey; and one after another they refused to take him."

"How'd we happen to get him, then?" queried one of our party.

"He showed up at San Francisco, neat as a new pin; exhibited several fine discharges, but said nothing of the last two, and was taken into the regiment as we were going through. Of course, its pretty much as they said in the First when we're in garrison, but, once out scouting, days away from a drop of 'tanglefoot,' and he does first rate. That's how he got his corporal's chevrons."

"He'll lose 'em again before we're back at Sandy forty-eight hours," growled Blake, strolling up to the party again.

But he did not. Prophecies failed this time, and old Potts wore those chevrons to the last.

He was a good prophet and a keen judge of human nature as exemplified in Gleason, who said that "the old man" was planning for a visit to the new ranches above Fort Phœnix. A day or two farther we plodded along down the range, our Indian scouts looking reproachfully—even sullenly—at the commander at every halt, and then came the order to turn back. Two marches more, and the little command went into bivouac close under the eaves of Fort Phœnix and we were exchanging jovial greetings with our brother officers at the post. Turning over the command to Lieutenant Blake, Mr. Gleason went up into the garrison with his own particular pack-mule; billeted himself on the infantry commanding officer—the major—and in a short time appeared freshly-shaved and in the neatest possible undress uniform, ready to call upon the few ladies at the post, and of course to make frequent reference to "my battalion," or "my command," down beyond the dusty, dismal corrals. The rest of us, having come out for business, had no uniforms, nothing but the rough field, scouting rig we wore on such duty, and every man's chin was bristling with a two-weeks'-old beard.

"I'm going to report Gleason for this thing," swore Blake; "you see if I don't, the moment we get back."

The rest of us were "hopping mad," too, but held our tongues so long as we were around Phœnix. We did not want them there to believe there was dissension and almost mutiny impending. Some of us got permission from Blake to go up to the post with its hospitable officers, and I was one who strolled up to "the store" after dark. There we found the major, and Captain Frazer, and Captain Jennings, and most of the youngsters, but Baker was absent. Of course the talk soon drifted to and settled on "Starlight Ranch," and by tattoo most of the garrison crowd were talking like so many Prussians, all at top-voice and all at once. Every man seemed to have some theory of his own with regard to the peculiar conduct of Mr. Burnham, but no one dissented from the quiet remark of Captain Frazer:

"As for Baker's relations with the daughter, he is simply desperately in love and means to marry her. He tells my wife that she is educated and far more refined than her surroundings would indicate, but that he is refused audience by both Burnham and his wife, and it is only at extreme risk that he is able to meet his lady-love at all. Some nights she is entirely prevented from slipping out to see him."

Presently in came Gleason, beaming and triumphant from his round of calls among the fair sex, and ready now for the game he loved above all things on earth,— poker. For reasons which need not be elaborated here no officer in our command would play with him, and an ugly rumor was going the rounds at Sandy, just before we came away, that, in a game at Olsen's ranch on the Aqua Fria about three weeks before, he had had his face slapped by Lieutenant Ray of our own regiment. But Ray had gone to his lonely post at Camp Cameron, and there was no one by whom we could verify it except some ranchmen, who declared that Gleason had cheated at cards, and Ray "had been a little too full," as they put it, to detect the fraud until it seemed to flash upon him all of a sudden. A game began, however, with three local officers as participants, so presently Carroll and I withdrew and went back to bivouac.

"Have you seen anything of Corporal Potts?" was the first question asked by Mr. Blake.

"Not a thing. Why? Is he missing?"

"Been missing for an hour. He was talking with some of these garrison soldiers here just after the men had come in from the herd, and what I'm afraid of is that he'll go up into the post and get bilin' full there. I've sent other non-commissioned officers after him, but they cannot find him. He hasn't even looked in at the store, so the bar-tender swears."

"The sly old rascal!" said Carroll. "He knows perfectly well how to get all the liquor he wants without exposing himself in the least. No doubt if the bar-tender were asked if he had not filled some flasks this evening he would say yes, and Potts is probably stretched out comfortably in the forage-loft of one of the stables, with a canteen of water and his flask of bug-juice, prepared to make a night of it."

Blake moodily gazed into the embers of the bivouac-fire. Never had we seen him so utterly unlike himself as on this burlesque of a scout, and now that we were virtually homeward-bound, and empty-handed too, he was completely weighed down by the consciousness of our lost opportunities. If something could only have happened to Gleason before the start, so that the command might have devolved on Blake, we all felt that a very different account could have been rendered; for with all his rattling, ranting fun around the garrison, he was a gallant and dutiful soldier in the field. It was now after ten o'clock; most of the men, rolled in their blankets, were sleeping on the scant turf that could be found at intervals in the half-sandy soil below the corrals and stables. The herds of the two troops and the pack-mules were all cropping peacefully at the hay that had been liberally distributed among them because there was hardly grass enough for a "burro." We were all ready to turn in, but there stood our temporary commander, his long legs a-straddle, his hands clasped behind him, and the flickering light of the fire betraying in his face both profound dejection and disgust.

"I wouldn't care so much," said he at last, "but it will give Gleason a chance to say that things always go wrong when he's away. Did you see him up at the post?" he suddenly asked. "What was he doing, Carroll?"

"Poker," was the sententious reply.

"What?" shouted Blake. "Poker? 'I thank thee, good Tubal,—good news,—good news!'" he ranted, with almost joyous relapse into his old manner. "'O Lady Fortune, stand you auspicious', for those fellows at Phœnix, I mean, and may they scoop our worthy chieftain of his last ducat. See what it means, fellows. Win or lose, he'll play all night, he'll drink much if it go agin' him, and I pray it may. He'll be too sick, when morning comes, to join us, and, by my faith, we'll leave his horse and orderly and march away without him. As for Potts,—an he appear not,—we'll let him play hide-and-seek with his would-be reformer. Hullo! What's that?"

There was a sound of alternate shout and challenge towards where the horses were herded on the level stretch below us. The sergeant of the guard was running rapidly thither as Carroll and I reached the corner of the corral. Half a minute's brisk spurt brought us to the scene.

"What's the trouble, sentry?" panted the sergeant.

"One of our fellows trying to take a horse. I was down on this side of the herd when I seen him at the other end trying to loose a side-line. It was just light enough by the moon to let me see the figure, but I couldn't make out who 'twas. I challenged and ran and yelled for the corporal, too, but he got away through the horses somehow. Murphy, who's on the other side of the herds, seen him and challenged too."

"Did he answer?"

"Not a word, sir."

"Count your horses, sergeant, and see if all are here," was ordered. Then we hurried over to Murphy's post.

"Who was the man? Could you make him out?"

"Not plainly, sir; but I think it was one of our own command," and poor Murphy hesitated and stammered. He hated to "give away," as he expressed it, one of his own troop. But his questioners were inexorable.

"What man did this one most look like, so far as you could judge?"

"Well, sir, I hate to suspicion anybody, but 'twas more like Corporal Potts he looked. Sure, if 'twas him, he must ha' been drinkin', for the corporal's not the man to try and run off a horse when he's in his sober sinses."

The waning moon gave hardly enough light for effective search, but we did our best. Blake came out and joined us, looking very grave when he heard the news. Eleven o'clock came, and we gave it up. Not a sign of the marauder could we find. Potts was still absent from the bivouac when we got back, but Blake determined to make no further effort to find him. Long before midnight we were all soundly sleeping, and the next thing I knew my orderly was shaking me by the arm and announcing breakfast. Reveille was just being sounded up at the garrison. The sun had not yet climbed high enough to peep over the Matitzal, but it was broad daylight. In ten minutes Carroll and I were enjoying our coffee and *frijoles;* Blake had ridden up into the garrison. Potts was still absent; and so, as we expected, was Mr. Gleason.

Half an hour more, and in long column of twos, and followed by our pack-train, the command was filing out along the road whereon "No. 3" had seen the ambulance darting by in the darkness. Blake had come back from the post with a flush of anger on his face and with lips compressed. He did not even dismount. "Saddle up at once" was all he said until he gave the commands to mount and march. Opposite the quarters of the commanding officer we were riding at ease, and there he shook his gauntleted fist at the whitewashed walls, and had recourse to his usual safety-valve,—

> "'Take heed, my lords, the welfare of us all
> Hangs on the cutting short that fraudful man,'

and may the devil fly away with him! What d'ye think he told me when I went to hunt him up?"

There was no suitable conjecture.

"He said to march ahead, leaving his horse, Potts's, and his orderly's, also the pack-mule: he would follow at his leisure. He had given Potts authority to wait and go with him, but did not consider it necessary to notify me."

"Where was he?"

"Still at the store, playing with the trader and some understrappers. Didn't seem to be drunk, either."

And that was the last we heard of our commander until late in the evening. We were then in bivouac on the west bank of the Sandy within short rifle-range of the buildings of Crocker's Ranch on the other side. There the lights burned brightly, and some of our people who had gone across had been courteously received, despite a certain constraint and nervousness displayed by the two brothers. At "Starlight," however, nearly a mile away from us, all was silence and darkness. We had studied it curiously as we marched up along the west shore, and some of the men had asked permission to fall out and ride over there, "just to see it," but Blake had refused. The Sandy was easily fordable on horseback anywhere, and the Crockers, for the convenience of their ranch people, had placed a lot of bowlders and heaps of stones in such position that they served as a foot-path opposite their corrals. But Blake said he would rather none of his people intruded at "Starlight," and so it happened that we were around the fire when Gleason rode in about nine o'clock, and with him Lieutenant Baker, also the recreant Potts.

"You may retain command, Mr. Blake," said the former, thickly. "I have an engagement this evening."

In an instant Baker was at my side. We had not met before since he was wearing the gray at the Point.

"For God's sake, don't let him follow me,—but *you*, —come if you possibly can. I'll slip off into the willows up-stream as soon as I can do so without his seeing."

I signalled Blake to join us, and presently he sauntered over our way, Gleason meantime admonishing his camp cook that he expected to have the very best hot supper for himself and his friend, Lieutenant Baker, ready in twenty minutes,—twenty minutes, for they had an important engagement, an *affaire de coor*, by Jove!

"You fellows know something of this matter," said Baker, hurriedly; "but I cannot begin to tell you how troubled I am. Something is wrong with *her*. She has not met me once this week, and the house is still as a grave. I must see her. She is either ill or imprisoned by her people, or carried away. God only knows why that hound Burnham forbids me the house. I cannot see him. I've never seen his wife. The door is barred against me and I cannot force an entrance. For a while she was able to slip out late in the evening and meet me down the hill-side, but they must have detected her in some way. I do not even know that she is there, but to-night I *mean* to know. If she is within those walls—and alive—she will answer my signal. But for heaven's sake keep that drunken wretch from going over there. He's bent on it. The major gave me leave again for to-night, provided I would see Gleason safely to your camp, and he has been maundering all the way out about how *he* knew more'n I did,—he and Potts, who's half-drunk too,—and how he meant to see me through in this matter."

"Well, here," said Blake, "there's only one thing to be done. You two slip away at once; get your horses, and ford the Sandy well below camp. I'll try and keep him occupied."

In three minutes we were off, leading our steeds until a hundred yards or so away from the fires, then mounting and moving at rapid walk. Following Baker's lead, I rode along, wondering what manner of adventure this was apt to be. I expected him to make an early crossing of the stream, but he did not. "The only fords I know," said he, "are down below Starlight," and so it happened that we made a wide *détour;* but during that dark ride he told me frankly how matters stood. Zoe Burnham had promised to be his wife, and had fully returned his love, but she was deeply attached to her poor mother, whose health was utterly broken, and who seemed to stand in dread of her father. The girl could not bear to leave her mother, though he had implored her to do so and be married at once. "She told me the last time I saw her that old Burnham had sworn to kill me if he caught me around the place, so I have to come armed, you see;" and he exhibited his heavy revolver. "There's something shady about the old man, but I don't know what it is."

At last we crossed the stream, and soon reached a point where we dismounted and fastened our horses among the willows; then slowly and cautiously began the ascent to the ranch. The slope here was long and gradual, and before we had gone fifty yards Baker laid his hand on my arm.

"Wait. Hush!" he said.

Listening, we could distinctly hear the crunching of horses' hoofs, but in the darkness (for the old moon was not yet showing over the range to the east) we could distinguish nothing. One thing was certain: those hoofs were going towards the ranch.

"Heavens!" said Baker. "Do you suppose that Gleason has got the start of us after all? There's no telling what mischief he may do. He swore he would stand inside those walls to-night, for there was no Chinaman on earth whom he could not bribe."

We pushed ahead at the run now, but within a minute I plunged into some unseen hollow; my Mexican spurs tangled, and down I went heavily upon the ground. The shock was severe, and for an instant I lay there half-stunned. Baker was by my side in the twinkling of an eye full of anxiety and sympathy. I was not injured in the slightest, but the breath was knocked out of me, and it was some minutes before I could forge ahead again. We reached the foot of the steep slope; we clambered painfully—at least I did—to the crest, and there stood the black outline of Starlight Ranch, with only a glimmer of light shining through the windows here and there where the shades did not completely cover the space. In front were three horses held by a cavalry trooper.

"Whose horses are these?" panted Baker.

"Lieutenant Gleason's, sir. Him and Corporal

Potts has gone round behind the ranch with a Chinaman they found takin' in water."

And then, just at that instant, so piercing, so agonized, so fearful that even the three horses started back snorting and terrified, there rang out on the still night air the most awful shriek I ever heard, the wail of a woman in horror and dismay. Then dull, heavy blows; oaths, curses, stifled exclamations; a fall that shook the windows; Gleason's voice commanding, entreating; a shrill Chinese jabber; a rush through the hall; more blows; gasps; curses; more unavailing orders in Gleason's well-known voice; then a sudden pistol shot, a scream of "Oh, my God!" then moans, and then silence. The casement on the second floor was thrown open, and a fair young face and form were outlined upon the bright light within; a girlish voice called, imploringly,—

"Harry! Harry! Oh, help, if you are there! They are killing father!"

But at the first sound Harry Baker had sprung from my side and disappeared in the darkness.

"We are friends," I shouted to her,—"Harry Baker's friends. He has gone round to the rear entrance." Then I made a dash for the front door, shaking, kicking, and hammering with all my might. I had no idea how to find the rear entrance in the darkness. Presently it was opened by the still chattering, jabbering Chinaman, his face pasty with terror and excitement, and the sight that met my eyes was one not soon to be forgotten.

A broad hall opened straight before me, with a stairway leading to the second floor. A lamp with burnished reflector was burning brightly midway down its length. Another just like it fully lighted a big room to my left,—the dining-room, evidently,—on the floor of which, surrounded by overturned chairs, was lying a woman in a deathlike swoon. Indeed, I thought at first she was dead. In the room to my right, only dimly lighted, a tall man in shirt-sleeves was slowly crawling to a sofa, unsteadily assisted by Gleason; and as I stepped inside, Corporal Potts, who was leaning against the wall at the other end of the room pressing his hand to his side and with ashen face, sank suddenly to the floor, doubled up in a pool of his own blood. In the dining-room, in the hall, everywhere that I could see, were the marks of a fearful struggle. The man on the sofa gasped faintly, " Water," and I ran into the dining-room and hastened back with a brimming goblet.

" What does it all mean?" I demanded of Gleason.

Big drops of sweat were pouring down his pallid face. The fearful scene had entirely sobered him.

" Potts has found the man who robbed him of his wife. That's she on the floor yonder. Go and help her."

But she was already coming to and beginning to stare wildly about her. A glass of water helped to revive her. She staggered across the hall, and then, with a moan of misery and horror at the sight, threw herself upon her knees, not beside the sofa where Burnham lay gasping, but on the floor where lay our poor old corporal. In an instant she had his head in her lap and was crooning over the senseless clay, swaying her body to and fro as she piteously called to him,—

c

"Frank, Frank! Oh, for the love of Jesus, speak to me! Frank, dear Frank, my husband, my own! Oh, for God's sake, open your eyes and look at me! I wasn't as wicked as they made me out, Frank, God knows I wasn't. I tried to get back to you, but Pierce there swore you were dead,—swore you were killed at Cieneguilla. Oh, Frank, Frank, open your eyes! *Do* hear me, husband. O God, don't let him die! Oh, for pity's sake, gentlemen, can't you do something? Can't you bring him to? He must hear me! He must know how I've been lied to all these years!"

"Quick! Take this and see if you can bring him round," said Gleason, tossing me his flask. I knelt and poured the burning spirit into his open mouth. There were a few gurgles, half-conscious efforts to swallow, and then—success. He opened his glazing eyes and looked up into the face of his wife. His lips moved and he called her by name. She raised him higher in her arms, pillowing his head upon her bosom, and covered his face with frantic kisses. The sight seemed too much for "Burnham." His face worked and twisted with rage; he ground out curses and blasphemy between his clinched teeth; he even strove to rise from the sofa, but Gleason forced him back. Meantime, the poor woman's wild remorse and lamentations were poured into the ears of the dying man.

"Tell me you believe me, Frank. Tell me you forgive me. O God! you don't know what my life has been with him. When I found out that it was all a lie about your being killed at Cieneguilla, he beat me like a slave. He had to go and fight in the war. They made him; they conscripted him; and when he got back he brought me papers to show you were killed in one of the Virginia battles. I gave up hope then for good and all."

Just then who should come springing down the stairs but Baker, who had evidently been calming and soothing his lady-love aloft. He stepped quickly into the parlor.

"Have you sent for a surgeon?" he asked.

The sound of his voice seemed to rouse "Burnham" to renewed life and raging hate.

"Surgeons be damned!" he gasped. "I'm past all surgery; but thank God I've given that ruffian what'll send him to hell before I get there! And you—*you*" —and here he made a frantic grab for the revolver that lay upon the floor, but Gleason kicked it away—" you, young hound, I meant to have wound you up before I got through. But I can jeer at you—God-forsaken idiot—I can triumph over you;" and he stretched forth a quivering, menacing arm and hand. "You *would* have your way—damn you!—so take it. You've given your love to a bastard,—that's what Zoe is."

Baker stood like one turned suddenly into stone. But from the other end of the room came prompt, wrathful, and with the ring of truth in her earnest protest, the mother's loud defence of her child.

"It's a lie,—a fiendish and malignant lie,—and he knows it. Here lies her father, my own husband, murdered by that scoundrel there. Her baptismal certificate is in my room. I've kept it all these years where he never could get it. No, Frank, she's your own, your own baby, whom you never saw. Go—go and bring her. He *must* see his baby-girl. Oh, my darling, don't—don't go until you see her." And again she covered the ashen face with her kisses. I knelt and put the flask to his lips and he eagerly swallowed a few drops. Baker had turned and darted upstairs. "Burnham's" late effort had proved too much for him. He had fainted away, and the blood was welling afresh from several wounds.

A moment more and Baker reappeared, leading his betrothed. With her long, golden hair rippling down her back, her face white as death, and her eyes wild with dread, she was yet one of the loveliest pictures I ever dreamed of. Obedient to her mother's signal, she knelt close beside them, saying no word.

"Zoe, darling, this is your own father; the one I told you of last winter."

Old Potts seemed struggling to rise; an inexpressible tenderness shone over his rugged, bearded face; his eyes fastened themselves on the lovely girl before him with a look almost as of wonderment; his lips seemed striving to whisper her name. His wife raised him still higher, and Baker reverently knelt and supported the shoulder of the dying man. There was the silence of the grave in the dimly-lighted room. Slowly, tremulously the arm in the old blue blouse was raised and extended towards the kneeling girl. Lowly she bent, clasping her hands and with the tears now welling from her eyes. One moment more and the withered old hand that for quarter of a century had grasped the sabre-hilt in the service of our common country slowly fell until it rested on that beautiful, golden head,—one little second or two, in which the lips seemed to murmur a prayer and the fast glazing eyes were fixed in infinite tenderness upon his only child. Then suddenly they sought the face of his sobbing wife,—a quick, faint smile, a sigh, and the hand dropped to the floor. The old trooper's life had gone out in benediction.

* * * * * * *

Of course there was trouble all around before that wretched affair was explained. Gleason came within an ace of court-martial, but escaped it by saying that he knew of "Burnham's" threats against the life of Lieutenant Baker, and that he went to the ranch in search of the latter and to get him out of danger. They met the Chinaman outside drawing water, and he ushered them in the back way because it was the nearest. Potts asked to go with him that he might see if this was his long-lost wife,—so said Gleason,— and the instant she caught sight of him she shrieked and fainted, and the two men sprang at each other like tigers. Knives were drawn in a minute. Then Burnham fled through the hall, snatched a revolver from its rack, and fired the fatal shot. The surgeon from Fort Phœnix reached them early the next morning, a messenger having been despatched from Crocker's ranch before eleven at night, but all his skill could not save "Burnham," now known to be Pierce, the ex-sutler clerk of the early Fifties. He had prospered and made money ever since the close of the war, and Zoe had been thoroughly well educated in the East before the poor child was summoned to share her mother's exile. His mania seemed to be to avoid all possibility of contact with the troops, but the Crockers had given such glowing accounts of the land near Fort Phœnix, and they were so positively assured that there need be no intercourse whatever with that post, that he determined to risk it. But, go where he would, his sin had found him out.

The long hot summer followed, but it often happened that before many weeks there were interchanges of visits between the fort and the ranch. The ladies insisted that the widow should come thither for change and cheer, and Zoe's appearance at Phœnix was the sensation of the year. Baker was in the seventh heaven. "Burnham," it was found, had a certain sense of justice, for his will had been made long before, and everything he possessed was left unreservedly to the woman whom he had betrayed and, in his tigerish way, doubtless loved, for he had married her in '65, the instant he succeeded in convincing her that Potts was really dead.

So far from combating the will, both the Crockers were cordial in their support. Indeed, it was the elder brother who told the widow of its existence. They had known her and her story many a year, and were ready to devote themselves to her service now. The junior moved up to the "Burnham" place to take general charge and look after matters, for the property was every day increasing in value. And so matters went until the fall, and then, one lovely evening, in the little wooden chapel at the old fort, there was a gathering such as its walls had never known before; and the loveliest bride that Arizona ever saw, blushing, smiling, and radiantly happy, received the congratulations of the entire garrison and of delegations from almost every post in the department.

A few years ago, to the sorrow of everybody in the

regiment, Mr. and Mrs. Harry Baker bade it good-by forever. The fond old mother who had so long watched over the growing property for "her children," as she called them, had no longer the strength the duties required. Crocker had taken unto himself a helpmate and was needed at his own place, and our gallant and genial comrade with his sweet wife left us only when it became evident to all at Phœnix that a new master was needed at Starlight Ranch.

WELL WON;

OR,

FROM THE PLAINS TO "THE POINT."

CHAPTER I.

RALPH McCREA.

THE sun was going down, and a little girl with big, dark eyes who was sitting in the waiting-room of the railway station was beginning to look very tired. Ever since the train came in at one o'clock she had been perched there between the iron arms of the seat, and now it was after six o'clock of the long June day, and high time that some one came for her.

A bonny little mite she was, with a wealth of brown hair tumbling down her shoulders and overhanging her heavy eyebrows. She was prettily dressed, and her tiny feet, cased in stout little buttoned boots, stuck straight out before her most of the time, as she sat well back on the broad bench.

She was a silent little body, and for over two hours had hardly opened her lips to any one,—even to the doll that now lay neglected on the seat beside her. Earlier in the afternoon she had been much engrossed with that blue-eyed, flaxen-haired, and overdressed beauty; but, little by little, her interest flagged, and when a six-year-old girlie loses interest in a brand-new doll something serious must be the matter.

Something decidedly serious was the matter now. The train that came up from Denver had brought this little maiden and her father,—a handsome, sturdy-looking ranchman of about thirty years of age,—and they had been welcomed with jubilant cordiality by two or three stalwart men in broad-brimmed slouch hats and frontier garb. They had picked her up in their brawny arms and carried her to the waiting-room, and seated her there in state and fed her with fruit and dainties, and made much of her. Then her father had come in and placed in her arms this wonderful new doll, and while she was still hugging it in her delight, he laid a heavy satchel on the seat beside her and said,—

"And now, baby, papa has to go up-town a ways. He has lots of things to get to take home with us, and some new horses to try. He may be gone a whole hour, but will you stay right here—you and dolly—and take good care of the satchel?"

She looked up a little wistfully. She did not quite like to be left behind, but she felt sure papa could not well take her,—he was always so loving and kind,—and then, there was dolly; and there were other children with their mothers in the room. So she nodded, and put up her little face for his kiss. He took her in his arms a minute and hugged her tight.

"That's my own little Jessie!" he said. "She's as brave as her mother was, fellows, and it's saying a heap."

With that he set her down upon the bench, and they

put dolly in her arms again and a package of apples within her reach; and then the jolly party started off.

They waved their hands to her through the window and she smiled shyly at them, and one of them called to a baggage-man and told him to have an eye on little Jessie in there. "She is Farron's kid."

For a while matters did not go so very badly. Other children, who came to look at that marvellous doll and to make timid advances, kept her interested. But presently the east-bound train was signalled and they were all whisked away.

Then came a space of over an hour, during which little Jessie sat there all alone in the big, bare room, playing contentedly with her new toy and chattering in low-toned, murmurous "baby talk" to her, and pointing out the wonderful sunbeams that came slanting in through the dust of the western windows. She had had plenty to eat and a big glass of milk before papa went away, and was neither hungry nor thirsty; but all the same, it seemed as if that hour were getting very, very long; and every time the tramp of footsteps was heard on the platform outside she looked up eagerly.

Then other people began to come in to wait for a train, and whenever the door opened, the big, dark eyes glanced quickly up with such a hopeful, wistful gaze, and as each new-comer proved to be a total stranger the little maiden's disappointment was so evident that some kind-hearted women came over to speak to her and see if all was right.

But she was as shy as she was lonely, poor little

mite, and hung her head and hugged her doll, and shrank away when they tried to take her in their arms. All they could get her to say was that she was waiting for papa and that her name was Jessie Farron.

At last their train came and they had to go, and a new set appeared; and there were people to meet and welcome them with joyous greetings and much homely, homelike chatter, and everybody but one little girl seemed to have friends. It all made Jessie feel more and more lonely, and to wonder what could have happened to keep papa so very long.

Still she was so loyal, so sturdy a little sentinel at her post. The kind-hearted baggage-man came in and strove to get her to go with him to his cottage "a ways up the road," where his wife and little ones were waiting tea for him; but she shook her head and shrank back even from him.

Papa had told her to stay there and she would not budge. Papa had placed his satchel in her charge, and so she kept guard over it and watched every one who approached.

The sun was getting low and shining broadly in through those western windows and making a glare that hurt her eyes, and she longed to change her seat. Between the sun glare and the loneliness her eyes began to fill with big tears, and when once they came it was so hard to force them back; so it happened that poor little Jessie found herself crying despite all her determination to be "papa's own brave daughter."

The windows behind her opened out to the north, and by turning around she could see a wide, level space between the platform and the hotel, where wagons and an omnibus or two, and a four-mule ambulance had been coming and going.

Again and again her eyes had wandered towards this space in hopeful search for father's coming, only to meet with disappointment. At last, just as she had turned and was kneeling on the seat and gazing through the tears that trickled down her pretty face, she saw a sight that made her sore little heart bound high with hope.

First there trotted into the enclosure a span of handsome bay horses with a low phaeton in which were seated two ladies; and directly after them, at full gallop, came two riders on spirited, mettlesome sorrels.

Little Jessie knew the horsemen at a glance. One was a tall, bronzed, dark-moustached trooper in the fatigue uniform of a cavalry sergeant; the other was a blue-eyed, faired-haired young fellow of sixteen years, who raised his cap and bowed to the ladies in the carriage, as he reined his horse up close to the station platform.

He was just about to speak to them when he heard a childish voice calling, "Ralph! Ralph!" and, turning quickly around, he caught sight of a little girl stretching out her arms to him through the window, and crying as if her baby heart would break.

In less time than it takes me to write five words he sprang from his horse, bounded up the platform into the waiting-room, and gathered the child to his heart, anxiously bidding her tell him what was the trouble.

For a few minutes she could only sob in her relief and joy at seeing him, and snuggle close to his face.

The ladies wondered to see Ralph McCrea coming towards them with a strange child in his arms, but they were all sympathy and loving-kindness in a moment, so attractive was her sweet face.

"Mrs. Henry, this is Jessie Farron. You know her father; he owns a ranch up on the Chugwater, right near the Laramie road. The station-master says she has been here all alone since he went off at one o'clock with some friends to buy things for the ranch and try some horses. It must have been his party Sergeant Wells and I saw way out by the fort."

He paused a moment to address a cheering word to the little girl in his arms, and then went on: "Their team had run away over the prairie—a man told us—and they were leading them in to the quartermaster's corral as we rode from the stables. I did not recognize Farron at the distance, but Sergeant Wells will gallop out and tell him Jessie is all right. *Would* you mind taking care of her a few minutes? Poor little girl!" he added, in lower and almost beseeching tones, "she hasn't any mother."

"*Would* I mind!" exclaimed Mrs. Henry, warmly. "Give her to me, Ralph. Come right here, little daughter, and tell me all about it," and the loving woman stood up in the carriage and held forth her arms, to which little Jessie was glad enough to be taken, and there she sobbed, and was soothed and petted and kissed as she had not been since her mother died.

Ralph and the station-master brought to the carriage the wonderful doll—at sight of whose toilet Mrs. Henry could not repress a significant glance at her lady friend, and a suggestive exclamation of "Horrors!"—and the heavy satchel. These were placed where Jessie could see them and feel that they were safe, and then she was able to answer a few questions and to look up trustfully into the gentle face that was nestled every little while to hers, and to sip the cup of milk that Ralph fetched from the hotel. She had certainly fallen into the hands of persons who had very loving hearts.

"Poor little thing! What a shame to leave her all alone! How long has her mother been dead, Ralph?" asked the other lady, rather indignantly.

"About two years, Mrs. Wayne. Father and his officers knew them very well. Our troop was camped up there two whole summers near them,—last summer and the one before,—but Farron took her to Denver to visit her mother's people last April, and has just gone for her. Sergeant Wells said he stopped at the ranch on the way down from Laramie, and Farron told him, then, he couldn't live another month without his little girl, and was going to Denver for her at once."

"I remember them well, now," said Mrs. Henry, "and we saw him sometimes when our troop was at Laramie. What was the last news from your father, Ralph, and when do you go?"

"No news since the letter that met me here. You know he has been scouting ever since General Crook went on up to the Powder River country. Our troop and the Grays are all that are left to guard that whole neighborhood, and the Indians seem to know it. They are 'jumping' from the reservation all the time."

"But the Fifth Cavalry are here now, and they will soon be up there to help you, and put a stop to all that,—won't they?"

"I don't know. The Fifth say that they expect orders to go to the Black Hills, so as to get between the reservations and Sitting Bull's people. Only six troops —half the regiment—have come. Papa's letter said I was to start for Laramie with them, but they have been kept waiting four days already."

"They will start now, though," said the lady. "General Merritt has just got back from Red Cloud, where he went to look into the situation, and he has been in the telegraph office much of the afternoon wiring to Chicago, where General Sheridan is. Colonel Mason told us, as we drove past camp, that they would probably march at daybreak."

"That means that Sergeant Wells and I go at the same time, then," said Ralph, with glistening eyes. "Doesn't it seem odd, after I've been galloping all over this country from here to the Chug for the last three years, that now father won't let me go it alone. I never yet set eyes on a war party of Indians, or heard of one south of the Platte."

"All the same they came, Ralph, and it was simply to protect those settlers that your father's company was there so much. This year they are worse than ever, and there has been no cavalry to spare. If you were my boy, I should be worried half to death at the idea of your riding alone from here to Laramie. What does your mother think of it?"

"It was mother, probably, who made father issue the order. She writes that, eager as she is to see me, she wouldn't think of letting me come alone with Sergeant Wells. Pshaw! He and I would be safer than the old stage-coach any day. That is never 'jumped' south of Laramie, though it is chased now and then above there. Of course the country's full of Indians between the Platte and the Black Hills, but we shouldn't be likely to come across any."

There was a moment's silence. Nestled in Mrs. Henry's arms the weary little girl was dropping off into placid slumber, and forgetting all her troubles. Both the ladies were wives of officers of the army, and were living at Fort Russell, three miles out from Cheyenne, while their husbands were far to the north with their companies on the Indian campaign, which was just then opening.

It was an anxious time. Since February all of the cavalry and much of the infantry stationed in Nebraska and Wyoming had been out in the wild country above the North Platte River, between the Big Horn Mountains and the Black Hills. For two years previous great numbers of the young warriors had been slipping away from the Sioux reservations and joining the forces of such vicious and intractable chiefs as Sitting Bull, Gall, and Rain-in-the-face, it could scarcely be doubted, with hostile intent.

Several thousands of the Indians were known to be at large, and committing depredations and murders in every direction among the settlers. Now, all pacific means having failed, the matter had been turned over to General Crook, who had recently brought the savage Apaches of Arizona under subjection, to employ such means as he found necessary to defeat their designs.

General Crook found the Sioux and their allies armed with the best modern breech-loaders, well supplied with ammunition and countless herds of war ponies, and far too numerous and powerful to be handled by the small force at his command.

One or two sharp and savage fights occurred in March, while the mercury was still thirty degrees below zero, and then the government decided on a great summer campaign. Generals Terry and Gibbon were to hem the Indians from the north along the Yellowstone, while at the same time General Crook was to march up and attack them from the south.

When June came, four regiments of cavalry and half a dozen infantry regiments were represented among the forces that scouted to and fro in the wild and beautiful uplands of Wyoming, Dakota, and Eastern Montana, searching for the Sioux.

The families of the officers and soldiers remained at the barracks from which the men were sent, and even at the exposed stations of Forts Laramie, Robinson, and Fetterman, many ladies and children remained under the protection of small garrisons of infantry. Among the ladies at Laramie was Mrs. McCrea, Ralph's mother, who waited for the return of her boy from a long absence at school.

A manly, sturdy fellow was Ralph, full of health and vigor, due in great part to the open-air life he had led in his early boyhood. He had "backed" an Indian pony before he was seven, and could sit one like a Comanche by the time he was ten. He had accompanied his father on many a long march and scout, and had ridden every mile of the way from the Gila River in Arizona, across New Mexico, and so on up into Nebraska.

He had caught brook trout in the Cache la Poudre,

and shot antelope along the Loup Fork of the Platte. With his father and his father's men to watch and keep him from harm, he had even charged his first buffalo herd and had been fortunate enough to shoot a bull. The skin had been made into a robe, which he carefully kept.

Now, all eager to spend his vacation among his favorite haunts,—in the saddle and among the mountain streams,—Ralph McCrea was going back to his army home, when, as ill-luck would have it, the great Sioux war broke out in the early summer of our Centennial Year, and promised to greatly interfere with, if it did not wholly spoil, many of his cherished plans.

Fort Laramie lay about one hundred miles north of Cheyenne, and Sergeant Wells had come down with the paymaster's escort a few days before, bringing Ralph's pet, his beautiful little Kentucky sorrel "Buford," and now the boy and his faithful friend, the sergeant, were visiting at Fort Russell, and waiting for a safe opportunity to start for home.

Presently, as they chatted in low tones so as not to disturb the little sleeper, there came the sound of rapid hoof-beats, and Sergeant Wells cantered into the enclosure and, riding up to the carriage, said to Ralph,—

"I found him, sir, all safe; but their wagon was being patched up, and he could not leave. He is so thankful to Mrs. Henry for her kindness, and begs to know if she would mind bringing Jessie out to the fort. The men are trying very hard to persuade him not to start for the Chug in the morning."

"Why not, sergeant?"

"Because the telegraph despatches from Laramie say

there must be a thousand Indians gone out from the reservation in the last two days. They've cut the wires up to Red Cloud, and no more news can reach us."

Ralph's face grew very pale.

"Father is right in the midst of them, with only fifty men!"

CHAPTER II.

CAVALRY ON THE MARCH.

It was a lovely June morning when the Fifth Cavalry started on its march. Camp was struck at daybreak, and soon after five o'clock, while the sun was still low in the east and the dew-drops were sparkling on the buffalo grass, the long column was winding up the bare, rolling "divide" which lay between the valleys of Crow and Lodge Pole Creeks. In plain view, only thirty miles away to the west, were the summits of the Rocky Mountains, but such is the altitude of this upland prairie, sloping away eastward between the two forks of the Platte River, that these summits appear to be nothing more than a low range of hills shutting off the western horizon.

Looking southward from the Laramie road, all the year round one can see the great peaks of the range— Long's and Hahn's and Pike's—glistening in their mantles of snow, and down there near them, in Colorado, the mountains slope abruptly into the Valley of the South Platte.

Up here in Wyoming the Rockies go rolling and billowing far out to the east, and the entire stretch of country, from what are called the "Black Hills of Wyoming," in contradistinction to the Black Hills of Dakota, far east as the junction of the forks of the Platte, is one vast inclined plane.

The Union Pacific Railway winds over these Black Hills at Sherman,—the lowest point the engineers could find,—and Sherman is over eight thousand feet above the sea.

From Sherman, eastward, in less than an hour's run the cars go sliding down with smoking brakes to Cheyenne, a fall of two thousand feet. But the wagon-road from Cheyenne to Fort Laramie twists and winds among the ravines and over the divides of this lofty prairie; so that Ralph and his soldier friends, while riding jauntily over the hard-beaten track this clear, crisp, sunshiny, breezy morning, were twice as high above the sea as they would have been at the tiptop of the Catskills and higher even than had they been at the very summit of Mount Washington.

The air at this height, though rare, is keen and exhilarating, and one needs no second look at the troopers to see how bright are their eyes and how nimble and elastic is the pace of their steeds.

The commanding officer, with his adjutant and orderlies and a little group of staff sergeants, had halted at the crest of one of these ridges and was looking back at the advancing column. Beside the winding road was strung a line of wires,—the military telegraph to the border forts,—and with the exception of those bare poles not a stick of timber was anywhere in sight.

The whole surface is destitute of bush or tree, but the thick little bunches of gray-green grass that cover it everywhere are rich with juice and nutriment. This is the buffalo grass of the Western prairies, and the moment the horses' heads are released down go their nozzles, and they are cropping eagerly and gratefully.

Far as the eye can see to the north and east it roams over a rolling, tumbling surface that seems to have become suddenly petrified. Far to the south are the snow-shimmering peaks; near at hand, to the west, are the gloomy gorges and ravines and wide wastes of upland of the Black Hills of Wyoming; and so clear is the air that they seem but a short hour's gallop away.

There is something strangely deceptive about the distances in an atmosphere so rare and clear as this.

A young surgeon was taking his first ride with a cavalry column in the wide West, and, as he looked back into the valley through which they had been marching for over half an hour, his face was clouded with an expression of odd perplexity.

"What's the matter, doctor?" asked the adjutant, with a grin on his face. "Are you wondering whether those fellows really are United States regulars?" and the young officer nodded towards the long column of horsemen in broad-brimmed slouch hats and flannel shirts or fanciful garb of Indian tanned buckskin. Even among the officers there was hardly a sign of the uniform or trappings which distinguish the soldiers in garrison.

"No, it isn't *that*. I knew that you fellows who had served so long in Arizona had got out of the way of wearing uniform in the field against Indians. What

I can't understand is that ridge over there. I thought we had been down in a hollow for the last half-hour, yet look at it; we must have come over that when I was thinking of something else."

"Not a bit of it, doctor," laughed the colonel. "That's where we dismounted and took a short rest and gave the horses a chance to pick a bit."

"Why, but, colonel! that must have been two miles back,—full half an hour ago: you don't mean that ridge is two miles away? I could almost hit that man riding down the road towards us."

"It would be a wonderful shot, doctor. That man is one of the teamsters who went back after a dropped pistol. He is a mile and a half away."

The doctor's eyes were wide open with wonder.

"Of course you must know, colonel, but it is incomprehensible to me."

"It is easily proved, doctor. Take these two telegraph poles nearest us and tell me how far they are apart."

The doctor looked carefully from one pole to another. Only a single wire was strung along the line, and the poles were stout and strong. After a moment's study he said, "Well, they are just about seventy-five yards apart."

"More than that, doctor. They are a good hundred yards. But even at your estimate, just count the poles back to that ridge—of course they are equidistant, or nearly so, all along—and tell me how far you make it."

The doctor's eyes began to dilate again as he silently took account of the number.

"I declare, there are over twenty to the rear of the wagon-train and nearly forty across the ridge! I give it up."

"And now look here," said the colonel, pointing out to the eastward where some lithe-limbed hounds were coursing over the prairie with Ralph on his fleet sorrel racing in pursuit. "Look at young McCrea out there where there are no telegraph poles to help you judge the distance. If he were an Indian whom you wanted to bring down what would you set your sights at, providing you had time to set them at all?" and the veteran Indian fighter smiled grimly.

The doctor shook his head.

"It is too big a puzzle for me," he answered. "Five minutes ago I would have said three hundred at the utmost, but I don't know now."

"How about that, Nihil?" asked the colonel, turning to a soldier riding with the head-quarters party.

Nihil's brown hand goes up to the brim of his scouting hat in salute, but he shook his head.

"The bullet would kick up a dust this side of him, sir," was the answer.

"People sometimes wonder why it is we manage to hit so few of these Cheyennes or Sioux in our battles with them," said the colonel. "Now you can get an idea of one of the difficulties. They rarely come within six hundred yards of us when they are attacking a train or an infantry escort, and are always riding full tilt, just as you saw Ralph just now. It is next to impossible to hit them."

"I understand," said the doctor. "How splendidly that boy rides!"

"Ralph? Yes. He's a genuine trooper. Now, there's a boy whose whole ambition is to go to West Point. He's a manly, truthful, dutiful young fellow, born and raised in the army, knows the plains by heart, and just the one to make a brilliant and valuable cavalry officer, but there isn't a ghost of a chance for him."

"Why not?"

"Why not? Why! how is he to get an appointment? If he had a home somewhere in the East, and his father had influence with the Congressman of the district, it might be done; but the sons of army officers have really very little chance. The President used to have ten appointments a year, but Congress took them away from him. They thought there were too many cadets at the Point; but while they were virtuously willing to reduce somebody else's prerogatives in that line, it did not occur to them that they might trim a little on their own. Now the President is allowed only ten 'all told,' and can appoint no boy until some of his ten are graduated or otherwise disposed of. It really gives him only two or three appointments a year, and he has probably a thousand applicants for every one. What chance has an army boy in Wyoming against the son of some fellow with Senators and Representatives at his back in Washington? If the army could name an occasional candidate, a boy like Ralph would be sure to go, and we would have more soldiers and fewer scientists in the cavalry."

By this time the head of the compact column was well up, and the captain of the leading troop, riding with his first lieutenant in front of his sets of fours, looked inquiringly at the colonel, as though half expectant of a signal to halt or change the gait. Receiving none, and seeing that the colonel had probably stopped to look over his command, the senior troop leader pushed steadily on.

Behind him, four abreast, came the dragoons,—a stalwart, sunburned, soldierly-looking lot. Not a particle of show or glitter in their attire or equipment. Utterly unlike the dazzling hussars of England or the European continent, when the troopers of the United States are out on the broad prairies of the West "for business," as they put it, hardly a brass button, even, is to be seen.

The colonel notes with satisfaction the nimble, active pace of the horses as they go by at rapid walk, and the easy seat of the men in their saddles.

First the bays of "K" Troop trip quickly past; then the beautiful, sleek grays of "B," Captain Montgomery's company; then more bays in "I" and "A" and "D," and then some sixty-five blacks, "C" Troop's color.

There are two sorrel troops in the regiment and more bays, and later in the year, when new horses were obtained, the Fifth had a roan and a dark-brown troop; but in June, when they were marching up to take their part in the great campaign that followed, only two of their companies were not mounted on bright bay horses, and one and all they were in the pink of condition and eager for a burst "'cross country."

It was, however, their colonel's desire to take them to their destination in good trim, and he permitted no "larking."

They had several hundred miles of weary marching before them. Much of the country beyond the Platte was "Bad Lands," where the grass is scant and poor, the soil ashen and spongy, and the water densely alkaline. All this would tell very sensibly upon the condition of horses that all winter long had been comfortably stabled, regularly groomed and grain-fed, and watered only in pure running streams flushed by springs or melting snow.

It was all very well for young Ralph to be coursing about on his fleet, elastic sorrel, radiant with delight as the boy was at being again "out on the plains" and in the saddle; but the cavalry commander's first care must be to bring his horses to the scene of action in the most effective state of health and soundness. The first few days' marching, therefore, had to be watched with the utmost care.

As the noon hour approached, the doctor noted how the hills off to the west seemed to be growing higher, and that there were broader vistas of wide ranges of barren slopes to the east and north.

The colonel was riding some distance ahead of the battalion, his little escort close beside, and Ralph was giving Buford a resting spell, and placidly ambling alongside the doctor.

Sergeant Wells was riding somewhere in the column with some chum of old days. He belonged to another regiment, but knew the Fifth of old. The hounds had tired of chasing over a waterless country, and with lolling tongues were trotting behind their masters' horses.

The doctor was vastly interested in what he had

heard of Ralph, and engaged him in talk. Just as they came in sight of the broad, open valley in which runs the sparkling Lodge Pole, a two-horse wagon rumbled up alongside, and there on the front seat was Farron, the ranchman, with bright-eyed, bonny-faced little Jessie smiling beside him.

"We've caught you, Ralph," he laughed, "though we left Russell an hour or more behind you. I s'pose you'll all camp at Lodge Pole for the night. We're going on to the Chug."

"Hadn't you better see the colonel about that?" asked Ralph, anxiously.

"Oh, it's all right! I got telegrams from Laramie and the Chug, both, just before we left Russell. Not an Indian's been heard of this side of the Platte, and your father's troop has just got in to Laramie."

"Has he?" exclaimed Ralph, with delight. "Then he knows I've started, and perhaps he'll come on to the Chug or Eagle's Nest and meet me."

"More'n likely," answered Farron. "You and the sergeant had better come ahead and spend the night with me at the ranch."

"I've no doubt the colonel will let us go ahead with you," answered Ralph, "but the ranch is too far off the road. We would have to stay at Phillips's for the night. What say you, sergeant?" he asked, as Wells came loping up alongside.

"The very plan, I think. Somebody will surely come ahead to meet us, and we can make Laramie two days before the Fifth."

"Then, good-by, doctor; I must ask the colonel first, but we'll see you at Laramie."

"Good-by, Ralph, and good luck to you in getting that cadetship."

"Oh, well! I *must* trust to luck for that. Father says it all depends on my getting General Sheridan to back me. If *he* would only ask for me, or if I could only do something to make him glad to ask; but what chance is there?"

What chance, indeed? Ralph McCrea little dreamed that at that very moment General Sheridan—far away in Chicago—was reading despatches that determined him to go at once, himself, to Red Cloud Agency; that in four days more the general would be there, at Laramie, and that in two wonderful days, meantime—but who was there who dreamed what would happen meantime?

CHAPTER III.

DANGER IN THE AIR.

WHEN the head of the cavalry column reached the bridge over Lodge Pole Creek a march of about twenty-five miles had been made, which is an average day's journey for cavalry troops when nothing urgent hastens their movements.

Filing to the right, the horsemen moved down the north bank of the rapidly-running stream, and as soon as the rearmost troop was clear of the road and beyond reach of its dust, the trumpets sounded "halt" and "dismount," and in five minutes the horses, unsaddled, were rolling on the springy turf, and then were driven out in herds, each company's by itself, to graze during the afternoon along the slopes. Each herd was watched and guarded by half a dozen armed troopers, and such horses as were notorious "stampeders" were securely "side-lined" or hobbled.

Along the stream little white tents were pitched as the wagons rolled in and were unloaded; and then the braying mules, rolling and kicking in their enjoyment of freedom from harness, were driven out and disposed upon the slopes at a safe distance from the horses. The smokes of little fires began to float into the air, and the jingle of spoon and coffee-pot and "spider" and skillet told that the cooks were busy getting dinner for the hungry campaigners.

Such appetites as those long-day marches give! Such delight in life and motion one feels as he drinks in that rare, keen mountain air! Some of the soldiers —old plainsmen—are already prone upon the turf, their heads pillowed on their saddles, their slouch hats pulled down over their eyes, snatching half an hour's dreamless sleep before the cooks shall summon them to dinner.

One officer from each company is still in saddle, riding around the horses of his own troop to see that the grass is well chosen and that his guards are properly posted and on the alert. Over at the road there stands a sort of frontier tavern and stage station, at which is a telegraph office, and the colonel has been sending despatches to Department Head-Quarters to announce the safe arrival of his command at Lodge Pole *en route* for Fort Laramie. Now he is talking with Ralph.

"It isn't that, my boy. I do not suppose there is

an Indian anywhere near the Chugwater; but if your father thought it best that you should wait and start with us, I think it was his desire that you should keep in the protection of the column all the way. Don't you?"

"Yes, sir, I do. The only question now is, will he not come or send forward to the Chug to meet me, and could I not be with mother two days earlier that way? Besides, Farron is determined to go ahead as soon as he has had dinner, and—I don't like to think of little Jessie being up there at the Chug just now. Would you mind my telegraphing to father at Laramie and asking him?"

"No, indeed, Ralph. Do so."

And so a despatch was sent to Laramie, and in the course of an hour, just as they had enjoyed a comfortable dinner, there came the reply,—

"All right. Come ahead to Phillips's Ranch. Party will meet you there at eight in the morning. They stop at Eagle's Nest to-night."

Ralph's eyes danced as he showed this to the colonel who read it gravely and replied,—

"It is all safe, I fancy, or your father would not say so. They have patrols all along the bank of the Platte to the southeast, and no Indians can cross without its being discovered in a few hours. I suppose they never come across between Laramie and Fetterman, do they, Ralph?"

"Certainly not of late years, colonel. It is so far off their line to the reservations where they have to run for safety after their depredations."

"I know that; but now that all but two troops of

cavalry have gone up with General Crook they might be emboldened to try a wider sweep. That's all I'm afraid of."

"Even if the Indians came, colonel, they've got those ranch buildings so loop-holed and fortified at Phillips's that we could stand them off a week if need be, and you would reach there by noon at latest."

"Yes. We make an early start to-morrow morning, and 'twill be just another twenty-five miles to our camp on the Chug. If all is well you will be nearly to Eagle's Nest by the time we get to Phillips's, and you will be at Laramie before the sunset-gun to-morrow. Well, give my regards to your father, Ralph, and keep your eye open for the main chance. We cavalry people want you for our representative at West Point, you know."

"Thank you for that, colonel," answered Ralph, with sparkling eyes. "I sha'n't forget it in many a day."

So it happened that late that afternoon, with Farron driving his load of household goods; with brown-haired little Jessie lying sound asleep with her head on his lap; with Sergeant Wells cantering easily alongside and Ralph and Buford scouting a little distance ahead, the two-horse wagon rolled over the crest of the last divide and came just at sunset in sight of the beautiful valley with the odd name of Chugwater.

Farther up the stream towards its sources among the pine-crested Black Hills, there were many places where the busy beavers had dammed its flow. The Indians, bent on trapping these wary creatures, had listened in the stillness of the solitudes to the battering of those wonderful tails upon the mud walls of their dams and forts, and had named the little river after its most marked characteristic, the constant "*chug, chug*" of those cricket-bat caudals.

On the west of the winding stream, in the smiling valley with tiny patches of verdure, lay the ranch with its out-buildings, corrals, and the peacefully browsing stock around it, and little Jessie woke at her father's joyous shout and pointed out her home to Ralph.

There where the trail wound away from the main road the wagon and horsemen must separate, and Ralph reined close alongside and took Jessie in his arms and was hugged tight as he kissed her bonny face. Then he and the sergeant shook hands heartily with Farron, set spurs to their horses, and went loping down northeastward to the broader reaches of the valley.

On their right, across the lowlands, ran the long ridge ending in an abrupt precipice, that was the scene of the great buffalo-killing by the Indians many a long year ago. Straight ahead were the stage station, the forage sheds, and the half dozen buildings of Phillips's. All was as placid and peaceful in the soft evening light as if no hostile Indian had ever existed.

Yet there were to be seen signs of preparation for Indian attack. The herder whom the travellers met two miles south of the station was heavily armed and his mate was only short rifle-shot away. The men waved their hats to Ralph and his soldier comrade, and one of them called out, "Whar'd ye leave the cavalry?" and seemed disappointed to hear they were as far back as Lodge Pole.

At the station, they found the ranchmen prepared for their coming and glad to see them. Captain McCrea had telegraphed twice during the afternoon and seemed anxious to know of their arrival.

"He's in the office at Laramie now," said the telegraph agent, with a smile, "and I wired him the moment we sighted you coming down the hill. Come in and send him a few words. It will please him more than anything I can say."

So Ralph stepped into the little room with its solitary instrument and lonely operator. In those days there was little use for the line except for the conducting of purely military business, and the agents or operators were all soldiers detailed for the purpose. Here at "The Chug" the instrument rested on a little table by the loop-hole of a window in the side of the log hut. Opposite it was the soldier's narrow camp-bed with its brown army blankets and with his heavy overcoat thrown over the foot. Close at hand stood his Springfield rifle, with the belt of cartridges, and over the table hung two Colt's revolvers.

All through the rooms of the station the same warlike preparations were visible, for several times during the spring and early summer war parties of Indians had come prowling up the valley, driving the herders before them; but, having secured all the beef cattle they could handle, they had hurried back to the fords of the Platte and, except on one or two occasions, had committed no murders.

Well knowing the pluck of the little community at Phillips's, the Indians had not come within long rifle range of the ranch, but on the last two visits the warriors seemed to have grown bolder. While most of the Indians were rounding up cattle and scurrying about in the valley, two miles below the ranch, it was noted that two warriors, on their nimble ponies, had climbed the high ridge on the east that overlooked the ranches in the valley beyond and above Phillips's, and were evidently taking deliberate note of the entire situation.

One of the Indians was seen to point a long, bare arm, on which silver wristlets and bands flashed in the sun, at Farron's lonely ranch four miles up-stream.

That was more than the soldier telegrapher could bear patiently. He took his Springfield rifle out into the fields, and opened a long range fire on these adventurous redskins.

The Indians were a good mile away, but that honest "Long Tom" sent its leaden missiles whistling about their ears, and kicking up the dust around their ponies' heels, until, after a few defiant shouts and such insulting and contemptuous gestures as they could think of, the two had ducked suddenly out of sight behind the bluffs.

All this the ranch people told Ralph and the sergeant, as they were enjoying a hot supper after the fifty-mile ride of the day. Afterwards the two travellers went out into the corral to see that their horses were secure for the night.

Buford looked up with eager whinny at Ralph's footstep, pricked his pretty ears, and looked as full of life and spirit as if he had never had a hard day's gallop in his life. Sergeant Wells had given him a careful rubbing down while Ralph was at the telegraph office, and later, when the horses were thoroughly cool, they were watered at the running stream and given a hearty feed of oats.

Phillips came out to lock up his stable while they were petting Buford, and stood there a moment admiring the pretty fellow.

"With your weight I think he could make a race against any horse in the cavalry, couldn't he, Mr. Ralph?" he asked.

"I'm not quite sure, Phillips: the colonel of the Fifth Cavalry has a horse that I might not care to race. He was being led along behind the head-quarters escort to-day. Barring that horse Van, I would ride Buford against any horse I've ever seen in the service for any distance from a quarter of a mile to a day's march."

"But those Indian ponies, Mr. Ralph, couldn't they beat him?"

"Over rough ground—up hill and down dale—I suppose some of them could. I saw their races up at Red Cloud last year, and old Spotted Tail brought over a couple of ponies from Camp Sheridan that ran like a streak, and there was a Minneconjou chief there who had a very fast pony. Some of the young Ogallallas had quick, active beasts, but, take them on a straight-away run, I wouldn't be afraid to try my luck with Buford against the best of them."

"Well, I hope you'll never have to ride for your life on him. He's pretty and sound and fast, but those Indians have such wind and bottom; they never seem to give out."

A little later—at about half after eight o'clock—Sergeant Wells, the telegraph operator, and one or two of the ranchmen sat tilted back in their rough chairs on the front porch of the station enjoying their pipes. Ralph had begun to feel a little sleepy, and was ready to turn in when he was attracted by the conversation between the two soldiers; the operator was speaking, and the seriousness of his tone caused the boy to listen.

"It isn't that we have any particular cause to worry just here. With our six or seven men we could easily stand off the Indians until help came, but it's Farron and little Jessie I'm thinking of. He and his two men would have no show whatever in case of a sudden and determined attack. They have not been harmed so far, because the Indians always crossed below Laramie and came up to the Chug, and so there was timely warning. Now, they have seen Farron's place up there all by itself. They can easily find out, by hanging around the traders at Red Cloud, who lives there, how many men he has, and about Jessie. Next to surprising and killing a white man in cold blood, those fellows like nothing better than carrying off a white child and concealing it among them. The gypsies have the same trait. Now, they know that so long as they cross below Laramie the scouts are almost sure to discover it in an hour or two, and as soon as they strike the Chug Valley some herders come tumbling in here and give the alarm. They have come over regularly every moon, since General Crook went up in February, *until now.*"

The operator went on impressively:

"The moon's almost on the wane, and they haven't shown up yet. Now, what worries me is just this. Suppose they *should* push out westward from the reservation, cross the Platte somewhere about Bull Bend or even nearer Laramie, and come down the Chug from the north. Who is to give Farron warning?"

"They're bound to hear it at Laramie and telegraph you at once," suggested one of the ranchmen.

"Not necessarily. The river isn't picketed between Fetterman and Laramie, simply because the Indians have always tried the lower crossings. The stages go through three times a week, and there are frequent couriers and trains, but they don't keep a lookout for pony tracks. The chances are that their crossing would not be discovered for twenty-four hours or so, and as to the news being wired to us here, those reds would never give us a chance. The first news we got of their deviltry would be that they had cut the line ten or twelve miles this side of Laramie as they came sweeping down.

"I tell you, boys," continued the operator, half rising from his chair in his earnestness, "I hate to think of little Jessie up there to-night. I go in every few minutes and call up Laramie or Fetterman just to feel that all is safe, and stir up Lodge Pole, behind us, to realize that we've got the Fifth Cavalry only twenty-five miles away; but the Indians haven't missed a moon yet, and there's only one more night of this."

Even as his hearers sat in silence, thinking over the soldier's words, there came from the little cabin the sharp and sudden clicking of the telegraph. "It's my call," exclaimed the operator, as he sprang to his feet and ran to his desk.

Ralph and Sergeant Wells were close at his heels; he had clicked his answering signal, seized a pencil, and was rapidly taking down a message. They saw his eyes dilate and his lips quiver with suppressed excitement. Once, indeed, he made an impulsive reach with his hand, as if to touch the key and shut off the message and interpose some idea of his own, but discipline prevailed.

"It's for you," he said, briefly, nodding up to Ralph, while he went on to copy the message.

It was a time of anxious suspense in the little office. The sergeant paced silently to and fro with unusual erectness of bearing and a firmly-compressed lip. His appearance and attitude were that of the soldier who has divined approaching danger and who awaits the order for action. Ralph, who could hardly control his impatience, stood watching the rapid fingers of the operator as they traced out a message which was evidently of deep moment.

At last the transcript was finished, and the operator handed it to the boy. Ralph's hand was trembling with excitement as he took the paper and carried it close to the light. It read as follows:

"RALPH McCREA, Chugwater Station:
"Black Hills stage reports having crossed trail of large war party going west, this side of Rawhide Butte. My troop ordered at once in pursuit. Wait for Fifth Cavalry.
"GORDON McCREA."

"Going west, this side of Rawhide Butte," said Ralph, as calmly as he could. "That means that they are twenty miles north of Laramie, and on the other side of the Platte."

"It means that they knew what they were doing

when they crossed just behind the last stage so as to give no warning, and that their trail was nearly two days old when seen by the down stage this afternoon. It means that they crossed the stage road, Ralph, but how long ago was that, do you think, and where are they now? It is my belief that they crossed the Platte above Laramie last night or early this morning, and will be down on us to-night."

"Wire that to Laramie, then, at once," said Ralph. "It may not be too late to turn the troop this way."

"I can only say what I think to my fellow-operator there, and can't even do that now; the commanding officer is sending despatches to Omaha, and asking that the Fifth Cavalry be ordered to send forward a troop or two to guard the Chug. But there's no one at the head-quarters this time o' night. Besides, if we volunteer any suggestions, they will say we were stampeded down here by a band of Indians that didn't come within seventy-five miles of us."

"Well, father won't misunderstand me," said Ralph, "and I'm not afraid to ask him to think of what you say; wire it to him in my name."

There was a long interval, twenty minutes or so, before the operator could "get the line." When at last he succeeded in sending his despatch, he stopped short in the midst of it.

"It's no use, Ralph. Your father's troop was three miles away before his message was sent. There were reports from Red Cloud that made the commanding officer believe there were some Cheyennes going up to attack couriers or trains between Fetterman and the Big Horn. He is away north of the Platte."

Another few minutes of thoughtful silence, then Ralph turned to his soldier friend,—

"Sergeant, I have to obey father's orders and stay here, but it's my belief that Farron should be put on his guard at once. What say you?"

"If you agree, sir, I'll ride up and spend the night with him."

"Then go by all means. I know father would approve it."

CHAPTER IV.

CUT OFF.

It was after ten o'clock when the waning moon came peering over the barrier ridge at the east. Over an hour had passed since Sergeant Wells, on his big sorrel, had ridden away up the stream on the trail to Farron's.

Phillips had pressed upon him a Henry repeating rifle, which he had gratefully accepted. It could not shoot so hard or carry so far as the sergeant's Springfield carbine, the cavalry arm; but to repel a sudden onset of yelling savages at close quarters it was just the thing, as it could discharge sixteen shots without reloading. His carbine and the belt of copper cartridges the sergeant left with Ralph.

Just before riding away he took the operator and Ralph to the back of the corral, whence, far up the valley, they could see the twinkling light at Farron's ranch.

"We ought to have some way of signalling," he had said as they went out of doors. "If you get news during the night that the Indians are surely this side of the Platte, of course we want to know at once; if, on the other hand, you hear they are nowhere within striking distance, it will be a weight off my mind and we can all get a good night's rest up there. Now, how shall we fix it?"

After some discussion, it was arranged that Wells should remain on the low porch in front of Farron's ranch until midnight. The light was to be extinguished there as soon as he arrived, as an assurance that all was well, and it should not again appear during the night unless as a momentary answer to signals they might make.

If information were received at Phillips's that the Indians were south of the Platte, Ralph should fire three shots from his carbine at intervals of five seconds; and if they heard that all was safe, he should fire one shot to call attention and then start a small blaze out on the bank of the stream, where it could be plainly seen from Farron's.

Wells was to show his light half a minute when he recognized the signal. Having arrived at this understanding, the sergeant shook the hand of Ralph and the operator and rode towards Farron's.

"What I wish," said the operator, "is that Wells could induce Farron to let him bring Jessie here for the night; but Farron is a bull-headed fellow and thinks no number of Indians could ever get the better of him and his two men. He knows very little of them and is hardly alive to the danger of his position.

I think he will be safe with Wells, but, all the same, I wish that a troop of the Fifth Cavalry had been sent forward to-night."

After they had gone back to the office the operator "called up" Laramie. "All quiet," was the reply, and nobody there seemed to think the Indians had come towards the Platte.

Then the operator signalled to his associate at Lodge Pole, who wired back that nobody there had heard anything from Laramie or elsewhere about the Indians; that the colonel and one or two of his officers had been in the station a while during the evening and had sent messages to Cheyenne and Omaha and received one or two, but that they had all gone out to camp. Everything was quiet; "taps" had just sounded and they were all going to bed.

"Lodge Pole" announced for himself that some old friends of his were on the guard that night, and he was going over to smoke a pipe and have a chat with them.

To this "Chug" responded that he wished he wouldn't leave the office. There was no telling what might turn up or how soon he'd be wanted.

But "Lodge Pole" said the operators were not required to stay at the board after nine at night; he would have the keeper of the station listen for his call, and would run over to camp for an hour; would be back at half-past ten and sleep by his instrument. Meantime, if needed, he could be called in a minute,— the guard tents were only three hundred yards away,— and so he went.

Ralph almost wished that he had sent a message to the colonel to tell him of their suspicions and anxiety.

He knew well that every officer and every private in that sleeping battalion would turn out eagerly and welcome the twenty-five-mile trot forward to the Chug on the report that the Sioux were out " on the war-path" and might be coming that way.

Yet, army boy that he was, he hated to give what might be called a false alarm. He knew the Fifth only by reputation, and while he would not have hesitated to send such a message to his father had he been camped at Lodge Pole, or to his father's comrades in their own regiment, he did not relish the idea of sending a despatch that would rout the colonel out of his warm blankets, and which might be totally unnecessary.

So the telegraph operator at Lodge Pole was permitted to go about his own devices, and once again Ralph and his new friend went out into the night to look over their surroundings and the situation.

The light still burned at Farron's, and Phillips, coming out with a bundle of kindling-wood for the little beacon fire, chuckled when he saw it,—

"Wells must be there by this time, but I'll just bet Farron is giving the boys a little supper, or something, to welcome Jessie home, and now he's got obstinate and won't let them douse the glim."

"It's a case that Wells will be apt to decide for himself," answered Ralph. "He won't stand fooling, and will declare martial law.—There! What did I tell you?"

The light went suddenly out in the midst of his words. They carried the kindling and made a little heap of dry sticks out near the bank of the stream;

then stood a while and listened. In the valley, faintly lighted by the moon, all was silence and peace; not even the distant yelp of coyote disturbed the stillness of the night. Not a breath of air was stirring. A light film of cloud hung about the horizon and settled in a cumulus about the turrets of old Laramie Peak, but overhead the brilliant stars sparkled and the planets shone like little globes of molten gold.

Hearing voices, Buford, lonely now without his friend, the sergeant's horse, set up a low whinny, and Ralph went in and spoke to him, patting his glossy neck and shoulder. When he came out he found that a third man had joined the party and was talking eagerly with Phillips.

Ralph recognized the man as an old trapper who spent most of his time in the hills or farther up in the neighborhood of Laramie Peak. He had often been at the fort to sell peltries or buy provisions, and was a mountaineer and plainsman who knew every nook and cranny in Wyoming.

Cropping the scant herbage on the flat behind the trapper was a lank, long-limbed horse from which he had just dismounted, and which looked travel-stained and weary like his master. The news the man brought was worthy of consideration, and Ralph listened with rapt attention and with a heart that beat hard and quick, though he said no word and gave no sign.

"Then you haven't seen or heard a thing?" asked the new-comer. "It's mighty strange. I've scoured these hills—man and boy—nigh onto thirty years and ought to know Indian smokes when I see 'em. I don't think I can be mistaken about this. I was way up the range about four o'clock this afternoon and could see clear across towards Rawhide Butte, and three smokes went up over there, sure. What startled me," the trapper continued, "was the answer. Not ten miles above where I was there went up a signal smoke from the foot-hills of the range,—just in here to the north-west of us, perhaps twenty miles west of Eagle's Nest. It's the first time I've seen Indian smokes in there since the month they killed Lieutenant Robinson up by the peak. You bet I came down. *Sure* they haven't seen anything at Laramie?"

"Nothing. They sent Captain McCrea with his troop up towards Rawhide just after dark, but they declare nothing has been seen or heard of Indians this side of the Platte. I've been talking with Laramie most of the evening. The Black Hills stage coming down reported trail of a big war party out, going west just this side of the Butte, and some of them may have sent up the smokes you saw in that direction. I was saying to Ralph, here, that if that trail was forty-eight hours old, they would have had time to cross the Platte at Bull Bend, and be down here to-night."

"They wouldn't come here first. They know this ranch too well. They'd go in to Eagle's Nest to try and get the stage horses and a scalp or two there. You're too strong for 'em here."

"Ay; but there's Farron and his little kid up there four miles above us."

"You don't tell me! Thought he'd taken her down to Denver."

"So he did, and fetched her back to-day. Sergeant Wells has gone up there to keep watch with them, and we are to signal if we get important news. All you tell me only adds to what we suspected. How I wish we had known it an hour ago! Now, will you stay here with us or go up to Farron's and tell Wells what you've seen?"

"I'll stay here. My horse can't make another mile, and you may believe I don't want any prowling round outside of a stockade this night. No, if you can signal to him go ahead and do it."

"What say you, Ralph?"

Ralph thought a moment in silence. If he fired his three shots, it meant that the danger was imminent, and that they had certain information that the Indians were near at hand. He remembered to have heard his father and other officers tell of sensational stories this same old trapper had inflicted on the garrison. Sergeant Wells himself used to laugh at "Baker's yarns." More than once the cavalry had been sent out to where Baker asserted he had certainly seen a hundred Indians the day before, only to find that not even the vestige of a pony track remained on the yielding sod. If he fired the signal shots it meant a night of vigil for everybody at Farron's and then how Wells would laugh at him in the morning, and how disgusted he would be when he found that it was entirely on Baker's assurances that he had acted!

It was a responsible position for the boy. He would much have preferred to mount Buford and ride off over the four miles of moonlit prairie to tell the sergeant of Baker's report and let him be the judge of its authenticity. It was lucky he had that level-headed soldier operator to advise him. Already he had begun to fancy him greatly, and to respect his judgment and intelligence.

"Suppose we go in and stir up Laramie, and tell them what Mr. Baker says," he suggested; and, leaving the trapper to stable his jaded horse under Phillips's guidance, Ralph and his friend once more returned to the station.

"If the Indians are south of the Platte," said the operator, "I shall no longer hesitate about sending a despatch direct to the troops at Lodge Pole. The colonel ought to know. He can send one or two companies right along to-night. There is no operator at Eagle's Nest, or I'd have him up and ask if all was well there. That's what worries me, Ralph. It was back of Eagle's Nest old Baker says he saw their smokes, and it is somewhere about Eagle's Nest that I should expect the rascals to slip in and cut our wire. I'll bet they're all asleep at Laramie by this time. What o'clock is it?"

The boy stopped at the window of the little telegraph room where the light from the kerosene lamp would fall upon his watch-dial. The soldier passed on around to the door. Glancing at his watch, Ralph followed on his track and got to the door-way just as his friend stretched forth his hand to touch the key.

"It's just ten-fifty now."

"Ten-fifty, did you say?" asked the soldier, glancing over his shoulder. "Ralph!" he cried, excitedly, "*the wire's cut!*"

"Where?" gasped Ralph. "Can you tell?"

"No, somewhere up above us,—near the Nest, probably,—though who can tell? It may be just round the bend of the road, for all we know. No doubt about there being Indians now, Ralph, give 'em your signal. Hullo! Hoofs!"

Leaping out from the little tenement, the two listened intently. An instant before the thunder of horse's feet upon wooden planking had been plainly audible in the distance, and now the coming clatter could be heard on the roadway.

Phillips and Baker, who had heard the sounds, joined them at the instant. Nearer and nearer came a panting horse; a shadowy rider loomed into sight up the road, and in another moment a young ranchman galloped up to the very doors.

" All safe, fellows? Thank goodness for that! I've had a ride for it, and we're dead beat. *Indians?* Why, the whole country's alive with 'em between here and Hunton's. I promised I'd go over to Farron's if they ever came around that way, but they may beat me there yet. How many men have you here?"

"Seven now, counting Baker and Ralph; but I'll wire right back to Lodge Pole and let the Fifth Cavalry know. Quick, Ralph, give 'em your signal now!"

Ralph seized his carbine and ran out on the prairie behind the corral, the others eagerly following him to note the effect. Bang! went the gun with a resounding roar that echoed from the cliffs at the east and came thundering back to them just in time to " fall in" behind two other ringing reports at short, five-second intervals.

Three times the flash lighted up the faces of the little party; set and stern and full of pluck they were. Then all eyes were turned to the dark, shadowy, low-lying objects far up the stream, the roofs of Farron's threatened ranch.

Full half a minute they watched, hearts beating high, breath coming thick and fast, hands clinching in the intensity of their anxiety.

Then, hurrah! Faint and flickering at first, then shining a few seconds in clear, steady beam, the sergeant's answering signal streamed out upon the night, a calm, steadfast, unwavering response, resolute as the spirit of its soldier sender, and then suddenly disappeared.

"He's all right!" said Ralph, joyously, as the young ranchman put spurs to his panting horse and rode off to the west. "Now, what about Lodge Pole?"

Just as they turned away there came a sound far out on the prairie that made them pause and look wonderingly a moment in one another's eyes. The horseman had disappeared from view. They had watched him until he had passed out of sight in the dim distance. The hoof-beats of his horse had died away before they turned to go.

Yet now there came the distant thunder of an hundred hoofs bounding over the sod.

Out from behind a jutting spur of a bluff a horde of shadows sweep forth upon the open prairie towards the trail on which the solitary rider has disappeared. Here and there among them swift gleams, like silver streaks, are plainly seen, as the moonbeams glint on armlet or bracelet, or the nickel plating on their gaudy trappings.

Then see! a ruddy flash! another! another! the muffled bang of fire-arms, and the vengeful yell and whoops of savage foeman float down to the breathless

f

listeners at the station on the Chug. The Sioux are here in full force, and a score of them have swept down on that brave, hapless, helpless fellow riding through the darkness alone.

Phillips groaned. "Oh, why did we let him go? Quick, now! Every man to the ranch, and you get word to Lodge Pole, will you?"

"Ay, ay, and fetch the whole Fifth Cavalry here at a gallop!"

But when Ralph ran into the telegraph station a moment later, he found the operator with his head bowed upon his arms and his face hidden from view.

"What's the matter,—quick?" demanded Ralph.

It was a ghastly face that was raised to the boy, as the operator answered,—

"It—it's all my fault. I've waited too long. *They've cut the line behind us!*"

CHAPTER V.

AT FARRON'S RANCH.

WHEN Sergeant Wells reached Farron's ranch that evening little Jessie was peacefully sleeping in the room that had been her mother's. The child was tired after the long, fifty-mile drive from Russell, and had been easily persuaded to go to bed.

Farron himself, with the two men who worked for him, was having a sociable smoke and chat, and the three were not a little surprised at Wells's coming and the unwelcome news he bore. The ranchman was one of the best-hearted fellows in the world, but he had a few infirmities of disposition and one or two little conceits that sometimes marred his better judgment. Having lived in the Chug Valley a year or two before the regiment came there, he had conceived it to be his prerogative to adopt a somewhat patronizing tone to its men, and believed that he knew much more about the manners and customs of the Sioux than they could possibly have learned.

The Fifth Cavalry had been stationed not far from the Chug Valley when he first came to the country, and afterwards were sent out to Arizona for a five-years' exile. It was all right for the Fifth to claim acquaintance with the ways of the Sioux, Farron admitted, but as for these fellows of the —th,—that was another thing. It did not seem to occur to him that the guarding of the neighboring reservations for about five years had given the new regiment opportunities to study and observe these Indians that had not been accorded to him.

Another element which he totally overlooked in comparing the relative advantages of the two regiments was a very important one that radically altered the whole situation. When the Fifth was on duty watching the Sioux, it was just after breech-loading rifles had been introduced into the army, and before they had been introduced among the Sioux.

Through the mistaken policy of the Indian Bureau at Washington this state of affairs was now changed and, for close fighting, the savages were better armed than the troops. Nearly every warrior had either a magazine rifle or a breech-loader, and many of them had two revolvers besides. Thus armed, the Sioux were about ten times as formidable as they had been before, and the task of restraining them was far more dangerous and difficult than it had been when the Fifth guarded them.

The situation demanded greater vigilance and closer study than in the old days, and Farron ought to have had sense enough to see it. But he did not. He had lived near the Sioux so many years; these soldiers had been near them so many years less; therefore they must necessarily know less about them than he did. He did not take into account that it was the soldiers' business to keep eyes and ears open to everything relating to the Indians, while the information which he had gained came to him simply as diversion, or to satisfy his curiosity.

So it happened that when Wells came in that night and told Farron what was feared at Phillips's, the ranchman treated his warning with good-humored but rather contemptuous disregard.

"Phillips gets stampeded too easy," was the way he expressed himself, "and when you fellows of the Mustangs have been here as long as I have you'll get to know these Indians better. Even if they did come, Pete and Jake here, and I, with our Henry rifles, could stand off fifty of 'em. Why, we've done it many a time."

"How long ago?" asked the sergeant, quietly.

"Oh, I don't know. It was before you fellows came. Why, you don't begin to know anything about these Indians! You never see 'em here nowadays, but when I first came here to the Chug there wasn't a week they didn't raid us. They haven't shown up in three years, except just this spring they've run off a little stock. But you never see 'em."

"*You* may never see them, Farron, but we do,—see them day in and day out as we scout around the reservation; and while I may not know what they were ten years ago, I know what they are *now*, and that's more to the purpose. You and Pete might have stood off a dozen or so when they hadn't 'Henrys' and 'Winchesters' as they have now, but you couldn't do it to-day, and it's all nonsense for you to talk of it. Of course, so long as you keep inside here you may pick them off, but look out of this window! What's to prevent their getting into your corral out there, and then holding you here! They can set fire to your roof over your head, man, and you can't get out to extinguish it."

"What makes you think they've spotted me, anyhow?" asked Farron.

"They looked you over the last time they came up the valley, and you know it. Now, if you and the men want to stay here and make a fight for it, all right, —I'd rather do that myself, only we ought to have two or three men to put in the corral,—but here's little Jessie. Let me take her down to Phillips's; she's safe there. He has everything ready for a siege and you haven't."

"Why, she's only just gone to sleep, Wells; I don't want to wake her up out of a warm bed and send her off four miles a chilly night like this,—all for a scare, too. The boys down there would laugh at me,—just after bringing her here from Denver, too."

"They're not laughing down there *this* night, Farron, and they're not the kind that get stampeded either. Keep Jessie, if you say so, and I'll stay through the night; but I've fixed some signals with them down at the road and you've got to abide by them. They can see your light plain as a beacon, and it's got to go out in fifteen minutes."

Farron had begun by pooh-poohing the sergeant's views, but he already felt that they deserved serious consideration. He was more than half disposed to adopt Wells's plan and let him take Jessie down to the safer station at Phillips's, but she looked so peaceful and bonny, sleeping there in her little bed, that he could not bear to disturb her. He was ashamed, too, of the appearance of yielding.

So he told the sergeant that while he would not run counter to any arrangement he had made as to signals, and was willing to back him up in any project for the common defence, he thought they could protect Jessie and the ranch against any marauders that might come along. He didn't think it was necessary that they should all sit up. One man could watch while the others slept.

As a first measure Farron and the sergeant took a turn around the ranch. The house itself was about thirty yards from the nearest side of the corral, or enclosure, in which Farron's horses were confined. In the corral were a little stable, a wagon-shed, and a poultry-house. The back windows of the stable were on the side towards the house, and should Indians get possession of the stable they could send fire-arrows, if they chose, to the roof of the house, and with their rifles shoot down any persons who might attempt to escape from the burning building.

This fault of construction had long since been pointed out to Farron, but the man who called his attention to it, unluckily, was an officer of the new regiment, and the ranchman had merely replied, with a self-satisfied smile, that he guessed he'd lived long enough in that country to know a thing or two about the Indians.

Sergeant Wells shook his head as he looked at the stable, but Farron said that it was one of his safeguards.

"I've got two mules in there that can smell an Indian five miles off, and they'd begin to bray the minute they did. That would wake me up, you see, because their heads are right towards me. Now, if they were way across the corral I mightn't hear 'em at all. Then it's close to the house, and convenient for feeding in winter. Will you put your horse in to-night?"

Sergeant Wells declined. He might need him, he said, and would keep him in front of the house where he was going to take his station to watch the valley and look out for signals. He led the horse to the stream and gave him a drink, and asked Farron to lay out a hatful of oats. "They might come in handy if I have to make an early start."

However lightly Farron might estimate the danger, his men regarded it as a serious matter. Having heard the particulars from Sergeant Wells, their first care was to look over their rifles and see that they were in perfect order and in readiness for use. When at last Farron had completed a leisurely inspection of his corral and returned to the house, he found Wells and

Pete in quiet talk at the front, and the sergeant's horse saddled close at hand.

"Oh, well!" he said, "if you're as much in earnest as all that, I'll bring my pipe out here with you, and if any signal should come, it'll be time enough then to wake Jessie, wrap her in a blanket, and you gallop off to Phillips's with her."

And so the watchers went on duty. The light in the ranch was extinguished, and all about the place was as quiet as the broad, rolling prairie itself. Farron remained wakeful a little while, then said he was sleepy and should go in and lie down without undressing. Pete, too, speedily grew drowsy and sat down on the porch, where Wells soon caught sight of his nodding head just as the moon came peeping up over the distant crest of the "Buffalo Hill."

How long Farron slept he had no time to ask, for the next thing he knew was that a rude hand was shaking his shoulder, and Pete's voice said,—

"Up with you, Farron! The signal's fired at Phillips's. Up quick!"

As Farron sprang to the floor, Pete struck a light, and the next minute the kerosene lamp, flickering and sputtering at first, was shining in the eastward window. Outside the door the ranchman found Wells tightening his saddle-girths, while his horse, snorting with excitement, pricked up his ears and gazed down the valley.

"Who fired?" asked Farron, barely awake.

"I don't know; Ralph probably. Better get Jessie for me at once. The Indians are this side of the Platte sure, and they may be near at hand. I don't like the way Spot's behaving,—see how excited he is. I don't like to leave you short-handed if there's to be trouble. If there's time I'll come back from Phillips's. Come, man! Wake Jessie."

"All right. There's plenty of time, though. They must be miles down the valley yet. If they'd come from the north, the telegraph would have given warning long ago. And Dick Warner—my brother-in-law, Jessie's uncle—always promised he'd be down to tell me first thing, if they came any way that he could hear of it. You bet he'll be with us before morning, unless they're between him and us now."

With that he turned into the house, and in a moment reappeared with the wondering, sleepy-eyed, half-wakened little maid in his strong arms. Wells was already in saddle, and Spot was snorting and prancing about in evident excitement.

"I'll leave the 'Henry' with Pete. I can't carry it and Jessie, too. Hand her up to me and snuggle her well in the blanket."

Farron hugged his child tight in his arms one moment. She put her little arms around his neck and clung to him, looking piteously into his face, yet shedding no tears. Something told her there was danger; something whispered "Indians!" to the childish heart; but she stifled her words of fear and obeyed her father's wish.

"You are going down to Phillips's where Ralph is, Jessie, darling. Sergeant Wells is going to carry you. Be good and perfectly quiet. Don't cry, don't make a particle of noise, pet. Whatever you do, don't make any noise. Promise papa."

As bravely as she had done when she waited that

day at the station at Cheyenne, the little woman choked back the rising sob. She nodded obedience, and then put up her bonny face for her father's kiss. Who can tell of the dread, the emotion he felt as he clung to the trusting little one for that short moment?

"God guard you, my baby," he muttered, as he carefully lifted her up to Wells, who circled her in his strong right arm, and seated her on the overcoat that was rolled at his pommel.

Farron carefully wrapped the blanket about her tiny feet and legs, and with a prayer on his lips and a clasp of the sergeant's bridle hand he bade him go. Another moment, and Wells and little Jessie were loping away on Spot, and were rapidly disappearing from view along the dim, moonlit trail.

For a moment the three ranchmen stood watching them. Far to the northeast a faint light could be seen at Phillips's, and the roofs and walls were dimly visible in the rays of the moon. The hoof-beats of old Spot soon died away in the distance, and all seemed as still as the grave. Anxious as he was, Farron took heart. They stood there silent a few moments after the horseman, with his precious charge, had faded from view, and then Farron spoke,—

"They'll make it all safe. If the Indians were anywhere near us those mules of mine would have given warning by this time."

The words were hardly dropped from his lips when from the other side of the house—from the stable at the corral—there came, harsh and loud and sudden, the discordant bray of mules. The three men started as if stung.

"Quick! Pete. Fetch me any one of the horses. I'll gallop after him. Hear those mules? That means the Indians are close at hand!" And he sprang into the house for his revolvers, while Pete flew round to the stable.

It was not ten seconds before Farron reappeared at the front door. Pete came running out from the stable, leading an astonished horse by the snaffle. There was not even a blanket on the animal's back, or time to put one there.

Farron was up and astride the horse in an instant, but before he could give a word of instruction to his men, there fell upon their ears a sound that appalled them,—the distant thunder of hundreds of bounding hoofs; the shrill, vengeful yells of a swarm of savage Indians; the crack! crack! of rifles; and, far down the trail along which Wells had ridden but a few moments before, they could see the flash of fire-arms.

"O God! save my little one!" was Farron's agonized cry as he struck his heels to his horse's ribs and went tearing down the valley in mad and desperate ride to the rescue.

Poor little Jessie! What hope to save her now?

CHAPTER VI.

A NIGHT OF PERIL.

For one moment the telegraph operator was stunned and inert. Then his native pluck and the never-say-die spirit of the young American came to his aid. He rose to his feet, seized his rifle, and ran out to join Phillips and the few men who were busily at work barricading the corral and throwing open the loopholes in the log walls.

Ralph had disappeared, and no one knew whither he had gone until, just as the men were about to shut the heavy door of the stable, they heard his young voice ring cheerily out through the darkness,—

"Hold on there! Wait till Buford and I get out!"

"Where on earth are you going?" gasped Phillips, in great astonishment, as the boy appeared in the doorway, leading his pet, which was bridled and saddled.

"Going? Back to Lodge Pole, quick as I can, to bring up the cavalry."

"Ralph," said the soldier, "it will never do. Now that Wells is gone I feel responsible for you, and your father would never forgive me if anything befell you. We can't let you go?"

Ralph's eyes were snapping with excitement and his cheeks were flushed. It was a daring, it was a gallant, thought,—the idea of riding back all alone through a country that might be infested by savage foes; but it was the one chance.

Farron and Wells and the men might be able to hold out a few hours at the ranch up the valley, and keep the Indians far enough away to prevent their burning them out. Of course the ranch could not stand a long siege against Indian ingenuity, but six hours, or eight at the utmost, would be sufficient time in which to bring rescue to the inmates. By that time he could have an overwhelming force of cavalry in the valley, and all would be safe.

If word were not sent to them it would be noon to-morrow before the advance of the Fifth would reach the Chug. By that time all would be over with Farron.

Ralph's brave young heart almost stopped beating as he thought of the hideous fate that awaited the occupants of the ranch unless help came to them. He felt that nothing but a light rider and a fast horse could carry the news in time. He knew that he was the lightest rider in the valley; that Buford was the fastest horse; that no man at the station knew all the "breaks" and ravines, the ridges and "swales" of the country better than he did.

Farron's lay to the southwest, and thither probably all the Indians were now riding. He could gallop off to the southeast, make a long *détour*, and so reach Lodge Pole unseen. If he could get there in two hours and a half, the cavalry could be up and away in fifteen minutes more, and in that case might reach the Chug at daybreak or soon afterwards.

One thing was certain, that to succeed he must go instantly, before the Indians could come down and put a watch around Phillips's.

Of course it was a plan full of fearful risk. He took his life in his hands. Death by the cruelest of tortures awaited him if captured, and it was a prospect before which any boy and many a man might shrink in dismay.

But he had thought of little Jessie; the plan and the estimation of the difficulties and dangers attending its execution had flashed through his mind in less than five seconds, and his resolution was instantly made. He was a soldier's son, was Ralph, and saying no word to any one he had run to the stable, saddled and bridled Buford, and with his revolver at his hip was ready for his ride.

"It's no use of talking; I'm going," was all he said. "I know how to dodge them just as well as any man here, and, as for father, he'd be ashamed of me if I didn't go."

Waiting for no reply,—before they could fully realize what he meant,—the boy had chirruped to his pawing horse and away they darted round the corner of the station, across the moonlit road, and then eastward down the valley.

"Phillips," exclaimed the soldier, "I never should have let him go. I ought to have gone myself; but he's away before a man can stop him."

"You're too heavy to ride that horse, and there's none other here to match him. That boy's got the sense of a plainsman any day, I tell you, and he'll make it all right. The Indians are all up the valley and we'll hear 'em presently at Farron's. He's keeping off so as to get round east of the bluffs, and then he'll strike across country southward and not try for the road until he's eight or ten miles away. Good for Ralph! It's a big thing he's doing, and his father will be proud of him for it."

But the telegraph operator was heavy-hearted. The men were all anxious, and clustered again at the rear of the station. All this had taken place in the space of three minutes, and they were eagerly watching for the next demonstration from the marauders.

Of the fate of poor Warner there could be little doubt. It was evident that the Indians had overwhelmed and killed him. There was a short struggle and the rapidly concentrating fire of rifles and revolvers for a minute or two; then the yells had changed to triumphant whoops, and then came silence.

"They've got his scalp, poor fellow, and no man could lend a hand to help him. God grant they're all safe inside up there at Farron's," said one of the party; it was the only comment made on the tragedy that had been enacted before them.

"Hullo! What's that?"

"It's the flash of rifles again. They've sighted Ralph!" cried the soldier.

"Not a bit of it. Ralph's off here to the eastward. They're firing and chasing up the valley. Perhaps Warner got away after all. *Look* at 'em! See! The flashes are getting farther south all the time! They've headed him off from Farron's, whoever it is, and he's making for the road. The cowardly hounds! There's a hundred of 'em, I reckon, on one poor hunted white man, and here we are with our hands tied!"

For a few minutes more the sound of shots and yells

and thundering hoofs came vividly through the still night air. All the time it was drifting away southward, and gradually approached the road. One of the ranchmen begged Phillips to let him have a horse and go out in the direction of the firing to reconnoitre and see what had happened, but it would have been madness to make the attempt, and the request was met with a prompt refusal.

"We shall need every man here soon enough at the rate things are going," was the answer. "That may have been Warner escaping, or it may have been one of Farron's men trying to get through to us or else riding off southward to find the cavalry. Perhaps it was Sergeant Wells. Whoever it was, they've had a two- or three-mile chase and have probably got him by this time. The firing in that direction is all over. Now the fun will begin up at the ranch. Then they'll come for us."

"It's my fault!" groaned the operator. "What a night,—and all my fault! I ought to have told them at Lodge Pole when I could."

"Tell them what?" said Phillips. "You didn't know a thing about their movements until Warner got here! What could you have said if you'd had the chance? The cavalry can't move on mere rumors or ideas that any chance man has who comes to the station in a panic. It has just come all of a sudden, in a way we couldn't foresee.

"All I'm worrying about now is little Jessie, up there at Farron's. I'm afraid Warner's gone, and possibly some one else; but if Farron can only hold out against these fellows until daylight I think he and his little one will be safe. Watch here, two of you, now, while I go back to the house a moment."

And so, arms at hand and in breathless silence, the little group watched and waited. All was quiet at the upper ranch. Farron's light had been extinguished soon after it had replied to the signal from below, but his roofs and walls were dimly visible in the moonlight. The distance was too great for the besiegers to be discerned if any were investing his place.

The quiet lasted only a few moments. Then suddenly there came from up the valley and close around those distant roofs the faint sound of rapid firing. Paled by the moonlight into tiny, ruddy flashes, the flame of each report could be seen by the sharper eyes among the few watchers at Phillips's. The attack had indeed begun at Farron's.

One of the men ran in to tell the news to Phillips, who presently came out and joined the party. No sign of Indians had yet been seen around them, but as they crouched there by the corral, eagerly watching the flashes that told of the distant struggle, and listening to the sounds of combat, there rose upon the air, over to the northward and apparently just at the base of the line of bluffs, the yelps and prolonged bark of the coyote. It died away, and then, far on to the southward, somewhere about the slopes where the road climbed the divide, there came an answering yelp, shrill, querulous, and prolonged.

"Know what that is, boys?" queried Phillips.

"Coyotes, I s'pose," answered one of the men,—a comparatively new hand.

"Coyotes are scarce in this neighborhood nowadays.

Those are Sioux signals, and we are surrounded. No man in this crowd could get out now. Ralph ain't out a moment too soon. God speed him! If Farron don't owe his life and little Jessie's to that boy's bravery, it'll be because nobody could get to them in time to save them. Why *didn't* he send her here?"

Bad as was the outlook, anxious as were all their hearts, what was their distress to what it would have been had they known the truth,—that Warner lay only a mile up the trail, stripped, scalped, gashed, and mutilated! Still warm, yet stone dead! And that all alone, with little Jessie in his arms, Sergeant Wells had ridden down that trail into the very midst of the thronging foe! Let us follow him, for he is a soldier who deserves the faith that Farron placed in him.

For a few moments after leaving the ranch the sergeant rides along at rapid lope, glancing keenly over the broad, open valley for any sign that might reveal the presence of hostile Indians, and then hopefully at the distant light at the station. He holds little Jessie in firm but gentle clasp, and speaks in fond encouragement every moment or two. She is bundled like a pappoose in the blanket, but her big, dark eyes look up trustfully into his, and once or twice she faintly smiles. All seems so quiet; all so secure in the soldier's strong clasp.

"That's my brave little girl!" says the sergeant. "Papa was right when he told us down at Russell that he had the pluckiest little daughter in all Wyoming. It isn't every baby that would take a night ride with an old dragoon so quietly."

He bends down and softly kisses the thick, curling

hair that hangs over her forehead. Then his keen eye again sweeps over the valley, and he touches his charger's flank with the spur.

"*Looks* all clear," he mutters, "but I've seen a hundred Indians spring up out of a flatter plain than that. They'll skulk behind the smallest kind of a ridge, and not show a feather until one runs right in among them. There might be dozens of them off there beyond the Chug at this moment, and I not be able to see hair or hide of 'em."

Almost half way to Phillips's, and still all is quiet. Then he notes that far ahead the low ridge, a few hundred yards to his left, sweeps round nearly to the trail, and dips into the general level of the prairie within short pistol-shot of the path along which he is riding. He is yet fully three-quarters of a mile from the place where the ridge so nearly meets the trail, but it is plainly visible now in the silvery moonlight.

"If they should have come down, and should be all ranged behind that ridge now, 'twould be a fearful scrape for this poor little mite," he thinks, and then, soldier-like, sets himself to considering what his course should be if the enemy were suddenly to burst upon him from behind that very curtain.

"Turn and run for it, of course!" he mutters. "Unless they should cut me off, which they couldn't do unless some of 'em were far back along behind the ridge. Hullo! A shadow on the trail! Coming this way. A horseman. That's good! They've sent out a man to meet me."

The sound of iron-shod hoofs that came faintly across the wide distance from the galloping shadow carried to the sergeant's practised ear the assurance that the advancing horseman was not an Indian. After the suspense of that lonely and silent ride, in the midst of unknown dangers, Wells felt a deep sense of relief.

"The road is clear between here and Phillips's, that's certain," he thought. "I'll take Jessie on to the station, and then go back to Farron's. I wonder what news that horseman brings, that he rides so hard."

Still on came the horseman. All was quiet, and it seemed that in five minutes more he would have the news the stranger was bringing,—of safety, he hoped. Jessie, at any rate, should not be frightened unless danger came actually upon them. He quickened his horse's gait, and looked smilingly down into Jessie's face.

"It's all right, little one! Somebody is coming up the trail from Phillips's, so everything must be safe," he told her.

Then came a cruel awakening. Quick, sudden, thrilling, there burst upon the night a mad chorus of shouts and shots and the accompaniment of thundering hoofs. Out from the sheltering ridge by dozens, gleaming, flashing through the moonlight, he saw the warriors sweep down upon the hapless stranger far in front.

He reined instantly his snorting and affrighted horse, and little Jessie, with one low cry of terror, tried to release her arms from the circling blanket and throw them about his neck; but he held her tight. He grasped the reins more firmly, gave one quick glance to his left and rear, and, to his dismay, discovered that he, too, was well-nigh hemmed in; that, swift and ruthless as the flight of hawks, a dozen warriors were bounding over the prairie towards him, to cut off his escape.

He had not an instant to lose. He whirled his practised troop horse to the right about, and sent him leaping madly through the night back for Farron's ranch.

Even as he sped along, he bent low over his charger's neck, and, holding the terror-stricken child to his breast, managed to speak a word to keep up her courage.

"We'll beat them yet, my bonny bird!" he muttered, though at that instant he heard the triumphant whoops that told him a scalp was taken on the trail behind him, though at that very instant he saw that warriors, dashing from that teeming ridge, had headed him; that he must veer from the trail as he neared the ranch, and trust to Farron and his men to drive off his pursuers.

Already the yells of his pursuers thrilled upon the ear. They had opened fire, and their wide-aimed bullets went whizzing harmlessly into space. His wary eye could see that the Indians on his right front were making a wide circle, so as to meet him when close to the goal, and he was burdened with that helpless child, and could not make fight even for his own life.

Drop her and save himself? He would not entertain the thought. No, though it be his only chance to escape!

His horse panted heavily, and still there lay a mile of open prairie between him and shelter; still those bounding ponies, with their yelping, screeching riders, were fast closing upon him, when suddenly through the dim and ghostly light there loomed another shadow, wild and daring,—a rider who came towards him at full speed.

Because of the daring of the feat to ride thus alone into the teeth of a dozen foemen, the sergeant was sure, before he could see the man, that the approaching horseman was Farron, rushing to the rescue of his child.

Wells shouted a trooper's loud hurrah, and then, "Rein up, Farron! Halt where you are, and open fire! That'll keep 'em off!"

Though racing towards him at thundering speed, Farron heard and understood his words, for in another moment his "Henry" was barking its challenge at the foe, and sending bullet after bullet whistling out across the prairie.

The flashing, feather-streaming shadows swerved to right and left, and swept away in big circles. Then Farron stretched out his arms,—no time for word of any kind,—and Wells laid in them the sobbing child, and seized in turn the brown and precious rifle.

"Off with you, Farron! Straight for home now. I'll keep 'em back." And the sergeant in turn reined his horse, fronted the foe, and opened rapid fire, though with little hope of hitting horse or man.

Disregarding the bullets that sang past his ears, he sent shot after shot at the shadowy riders, checked now, and circling far out on the prairie, until once more he could look about him, and see that Farron had reached the ranch, and had thrown himself from his horse.

Then slowly he turned back, fronting now and then

to answer the shots that came singing by him, and to hurrah with delight when, as the Indians came within range of the ranch, its inmates opened fire on them, and a pony sent a yelping rider flying over his head, as he stumbled and plunged to earth, shot through the body.

Then Wells turned in earnest and made a final dash for the corral. Then his own good steed, that had borne them both so bravely, suddenly wavered and tottered under him. He knew too well that the gallant horse had received his death-blow even before he went heavily to ground within fifty yards of the ranch.

Wells was up in an instant, unharmed, and made a rush, stooping low.

Another moment, and he was drawn within the doorway, panting and exhausted, but safe. He listened with amazement to the outward sounds of shots and hoofs and yells dying away into the distance southward.

"What on earth is that?" he asked.

"It's that scoundrel, Pete. He's taken my horse and deserted!" was Farron's breathless answer. "I hope they'll catch and kill him! I despise a coward!"

CHAPTER VII.

THE RESCUE.

ALL the time, travelling at rapid lope, but at the same time saving Buford's strength for sudden emergency, Ralph McCrea rode warily through the night. He kept far to east of the high ridge of the "Buffalo Hill,"—Who knew what Indian eyes might be watching there?—and mile after mile he wound among the ravines and swales which he had learned so well in by-gone days when he little dreamed of the value that his "plainscraft" might be to him.

For a while his heart beat like a trip-hammer; every echo of his courser's footfall seemed to him to be the rush of coming warriors, and time and again he glanced nervously over his shoulder, dreading pursuit. But he never wavered in his gallant purpose.

The long ridge was soon left to his right rear, and now he began to edge over towards the west, intending in this way to reach the road at a point where there would lie before him a fifteen-mile stretch of good "going ground." Over that he meant to send Buford at full speed.

Since starting he had heard no sound of the fray; the ridge and the distance had swallowed up the clamor; but he knew full well that the raiding Indians would do their utmost this night to burn the Farron ranch and kill or capture its inmates. Every recurring thought of the peril of his beleaguered friends prompted him to spur his faithful steed, but he had been reared in the cavalry and taught never to drive a willing horse to death.

The long, sweeping, elastic strides with which Buford bore him over the rolling prairie served their needs far better than a mad race of a mile or two, ending in a complete break-down, would have done.

At last, gleaming in the moonlight, he sighted the hard-beaten road as it twisted and wound over the slopes, and in a few moments more rode beneath the single wire of the telegraph line, and then gave Buford a gentle touch of the steel. He had made a circuit of ten miles or more to reach this point, and was now, he judged, about seven miles below the station and five miles from Farron's ranch.

He glanced over his right shoulder and anxiously searched the sky and horizon. Intervening "divides" shut him off from a view of the valley, but he saw that as yet no glare of flames proceeded from it.

"Thus far the defence has held its own," he said, hopefully, to himself. "Now, if Buford and I can only reach Lodge Pole unmolested there may yet be time."

Ascending a gentle slope he reined Buford down to a walk, so that his pet might have a little breathing spell. As he arrived at the crest he cast an eager glance over the next "reach" of prairie landscape, and then—his heart seemed to leap to his throat and a chill wave to rush through his veins.

Surely he saw a horseman dart behind the low mound off to the west. This convinced him that the Indians had discovered and pursued him. After the

Indian fashion they had not come squarely along his trail and thus driven him ahead at increased speed, but with the savage science of their warfare, they were working past him, far to his right, intending to head him off.

To his left front the country was clear, and he could see over it for a considerable distance. The road, after winding through some intermediate ravines ahead, swept around to the left. He had almost determined to leave the trail and make a bee-line across country, and so to outrun the foeman to his right, when, twice or thrice, he caught the gleam of steel or silver or nickel-plate beyond the low ground in the very direction in which he had thought to flee.

His heart sank low now, for the sight conveyed to his mind but one idea,—that the gleams were the flashing of moonbeams on the barbaric ornaments of Indians, as he had seen them flash an hour ago when the warriors raced forth into the valley of the Chug. Were the Indians ahead of him then, and on both sides of the road?

One thing he had to do, and to do instantly: ride into the first hollow he could find, dismount, crawl to the ridge and peer around him,—study which way to ride if he should have to make a race for his own life now,—and give Buford time to gather himself for the effort.

The boy's brave spirit was wrought well-nigh to the limit. His eyes clouded as he thought of his father and the faithful troop, miles and miles away and all unconscious of his deadly peril; of his anxious and loving mother, wakeful and watching at Laramie, doubtless informed of the Indian raid by this time; powerless to help him, but praying God to watch over her boy.

He looked aloft at the starry heavens and lifted his heart in one brief prayer : "God guard and guide me. I've tried to do my duty as a soldier's son." And somehow he felt nerved and strengthened.

He grasped the handle of his cavalry revolver as he guided Buford down to the right where there seemed to be a hollow among the slopes. Just as he came trotting briskly round a little shoulder of the nearest ridge there was a rush and patter of hoofs on the other side of it, an exclamation, half-terror, half-menace, a flash and a shot that whizzed far over his head. A dark, shadowy horseman went scurrying off into space as fast as a spurred and startled horse could carry him; a broad-brimmed slouch hat was blown back to him as a parting *souvenir*, and Ralph McCrea shouted with relief and merriment as he realized that some man—a ranchman doubtless—had taken him for an Indian and had " stampeded," scared out of his wits.

Ralph dismounted, picked up the hat, swung himself again into saddle, and with rejoicing heart sped away again on his mission. There were still those suspicious flashes off to the east that he must dodge, and to avoid them he shaped his course well to the west.

Let us turn for a moment to the camp of the cavalry down in Lodge Pole Valley. We have not heard from them since early evening when the operator announced his intention of going over to have a smoke and a chat with some of his friends on guard.

"Taps," the signal to extinguish lights and go to bed, had sounded early and, so far as the operator at Lodge Pole knew when he closed his instrument, the battalion had gladly obeyed the summons.

It happened, however, that the colonel had been talking with one of his most trusted captains as they left the office a short time before, and the result of that brief talk was that the latter walked briskly away towards the bivouac fires of his troop and called "Sergeant Stauffer!"

A tall, dark-eyed, bronzed trooper quickly arose, dropped his pipe, and strode over to where his captain stood in the flickering light, and, saluting, "stood attention" and waited.

"Sergeant, let the quartermaster-sergeant and six men stay here to load our baggage in the morning. Mount the rest of the troop at once, without any noise,—fully equipped."

The sergeant was too old a soldier even to look surprised. In fifteen minutes, with hardly a sound of unusual preparation, fifty horsemen had "led into line," had mounted, and were riding silently off northward. The colonel said to the captain, as he gave him a word of good-by,—

"I don't know that you'll find anything out of the way at all, but, with such indications, I believe it best to throw forward a small force to look after the Chug Valley until we come up. We'll be with you by dinner-time."

Two hours later, when the telegraph operator, breathless and excited, rushed into the colonel's tent and woke him with the news that his wire was cut up towards the Chug, the colonel was devoutly thankful for the inspiration that prompted him to send "K" Troop forward through the darkness. He bade his adjutant, the light-weight of the officers then on duty, take his own favorite racer, Van, and speed away on the trail of "K" Troop, tell them that the line was cut,—that there was trouble ahead; to push on lively with what force they had, and that two more companies would be hurried to their support.

At midnight "K" Troop, riding easily along in the moonlight, had travelled a little over half the distance to Phillips's ranch. The lieutenant, who with two or three troopers was scouting far in advance, halted at the crest of a high ridge over which the road climbs, and dismounted his little party for a brief rest while he went up ahead to reconnoitre.

Cavalrymen in the Indian country never ride into full view on top of a "divide" until after some one of their number has carefully looked over the ground beyond.

There was nothing in sight that gave cause for long inspection, or that warranted the officer's taking out his field-glasses. He could see the line of hills back of the Chugwater Valley, and all was calm and placid. The valley itself lay some hundreds of feet below his point of observation, and beginning far off to his left ran northeastward until one of its branches crossed the trail along which the troop was riding.

Returning to his party, the lieutenant's eye was attracted, for the fifth or sixth time since they had left Lodge Pole, by little gleams and flashes of light off in the distance, and he muttered, in a somewhat disparaging manner, to some of the members of his own troop,—

"Now, what the dickens can those men be carrying to make such a streak as that? One would suppose that Arizona would have taken all the nonsense out of 'em, but that glimmer must come from bright bits or buckles, or something of the kind, for we haven't a sabre with us. What makes those little flashes, sergeant?" he asked, impatiently.

"It's some of the tin canteens, sir. The cloth is all worn off a dozen of 'em, and when the moonlight strikes 'em it makes a flash almost like a mirror."

"Indeed it does, and would betray our coming miles away of a moonlit night. We'll drop all those things at Laramie. Hullo! Mount, men, lively!"

The young officer and his party suddenly sprang to saddle. A clatter of distant hoofs was heard rapidly approaching along the hard-beaten road. Nearer, nearer they came at tearing gallop. The lieutenant rode cautiously forward to where he could peer over the crest.

"Somebody riding like mad!" he muttered. "Hatless and demoralized. Who comes *there?*" he shouted aloud. "Halt, whoever you are!"

Pulling up a panting horse, pale, wide-eyed, almost exhausted, a young ranchman rode into the midst of the group. It was half a minute before he could speak. When at last he recovered breath, it was a marvellous tale that he told.

"The Chug's crammed with Indians. They've killed all down at Phillips's, and got all around Farron's,—hundreds of 'em. Sergeant Wells tried to run away with Jessie, but they cut him off, and he'd have been killed and Jessie captured but for me and Farron. We charged through 'em, and got 'em back to the ranch. Then the Indians attacked us there, and there was only four of us, and some one had to cut his way out. Wells said you fellows were down at Lodge Pole, but he da'sn't try it. I had to." Here "Pete" looked important, and gave his pistol-belt a hitch.

"I must 'a' killed six of 'em," he continued. "Both my revolvers empty, and I dropped one of 'em on the trail. My hat was shot clean off my head, but they missed me, and I got through. They chased me every inch of the way up to a mile back over yonder. I shot the last one there. But how many men you got?"

"About fifty," answered the lieutenant. "We'll push ahead at once. You guide us."

"I ain't going ahead with no fifty. I tell you there's a thousand Indians there. Where's the rest of the regiment?"

"Back at Lodge Pole. Go on, if you like, and tell them your story. Here's the captain now."

With new and imposing additions, Pete told the story a second time. Barely waiting to hear it through, the captain's voice rang along the eager column,—

"Forward, trot, *march!*"

Away went the troop full tilt for the Chug, while the ranchman rode rearward until he met the supporting squadron two hours behind. Ten minutes after parting with their informant, the officers of "K" Troop, well out in front of their men, caught sight of a daring horseman sweeping at full gallop down from some high bluffs to their left and front.

"Rides like an Indian," said the captain; "but no Sioux would come down at us like that, waving a hat, too. By Jupiter! It's Ralph McCrea! How are you, boy? What's wrong at the Chug?"

"Farron's surrounded, and I believe Warner's killed!" said Ralph, breathless. "Thank God, you're here so far ahead of where I expected to find you! We'll get there in time now;" and he turned his panting horse and rode eagerly along by the captain's side.

"And you've not been chased? You've seen nobody?" was the lieutenant's question.

"Nobody but a white man, worse scared than I was, who left his hat behind when I ran upon him a mile back here."

Even in the excitement and urgent haste of the moment, there went up a shout of laughter at the expense of Pete; but as they reached the next divide, and got another look well to the front, the laughter gave place to the grinding of teeth and muttered malediction. A broad glare was in the northern sky, and smoke and flame were rolling up from the still distant valley of the Chug, and now the word was "Gallop!"

Fifteen minutes of hard, breathless riding followed. Horses snorted and plunged in eager race with their fellows; officers warned even as they galloped, "Steady, there! Keep back! Keep your places, men!" Bearded, bright-eyed troopers, with teeth set hard together and straining muscles, grasped their ready carbines, and thrust home the grim copper cartridges. On and on, as the flaring beacon grew redder and fiercer ahead; on and on, until they were almost at the valley's edge, and then young Ralph, out at the front with the veteran captain, panted to him, in wild excitement that he strove manfully to control,—

"Now keep well over to the left, captain! I know the ground well. It's all open. We can sweep down from behind that ridge, and they'll never look for us or think of us till we're right among them. Hear them yell!"

"Ay, ay, Ralph! Lead the way. Ready now, men!" He turned in his saddle. "Not a word till I order 'Charge!' Then yell all you want to."

Down into the ravine they thunder; round the moonlit slope they sweep; swift they gallop through the shadows of the eastward bluffs; nearer and nearer they come, manes and tails streaming in the night wind; horses panting hard, but never flagging.

Listen! Hear those shots and yells and war-whoops! Listen to the hideous crackling of the flames! Mark the vengeful triumph in those savage howls! Already the fire has leaped from the sheds to the rough shingling. The last hope of the sore-besieged is gone.

Then, with sudden blare of trumpet, with ringing cheer, with thundering hoof and streaming pennon and thrilling rattle of carbine and pistol; with one magnificent, triumphant burst of speed the troop comes whirling out from the covert of the bluff and sweeps all before it down the valley.

Away go Sioux and Cheyenne; away, yelling shrill warning, go warrior and chief; away, down stream, past the stiffening form of the brave fellow they killed; away past the station where the loop-holes blaze with rifle-shots and ring with exultant cheers; away across the road and down the winding valley, and so far to the north and the sheltering arms of the reservation,— and one more Indian raid is over.

But at the ranch, while willing hands were dashing water on the flames, Ralph and the lieutenant sprang inside the door-way just as Farron lifted from a deep, cellar-like aperture in the middle of the floor a sobbing yet wonderfully happy little maiden. She clung to him hysterically, as he shook hands with one after another of the few rescuers who had time to hurry in.

Wells, with bandaged head and arm, was sitting at his post, his "Henry" still between his knees, and he looked volumes of pride and delight into his young friend's sparkling eyes. Pete, of course, was nowhere to be seen. Jake, with a rifle-bullet through his shoulder, was grinning pale gratification at the troopers who came in, and then there was a moment's silence as the captain entered.

Farron stepped forward and held forth his hand. Tears were starting from his eyes.

"You've saved me and my little girl, captain. I never can thank you enough."

"Bosh! Never mind us. Where's Ralph McCrea? There's the boy you can thank for it all. *He* led us?"

And though hot blushes sprang to the youngster's cheeks, and he, too, would have disclaimed any credit for the rescue, the soldiers would not have it so. 'Twas Ralph who dared that night-ride to bring the direful news; 'twas Ralph who guided them by the shortest, quickest route, and was with the foremost in the charge. And so, a minute after, when Farron unclasped little Jessie's arms from about his own neck, he whispered in her ear,—

" 'Twas Ralph who saved us, baby. You must thank him for me, too."

And so, just as the sun was coming up, the little girl with big, dark eyes whom we saw sitting in the railway station at Cheyenne, waiting wearily and patiently for her father's coming, and sobbing her relief and joy when she finally caught sight of Ralph, was once more nestling a tear-wet face to his and clasping him in her little arms, and thanking him with all her loyal, loving heart for the gallant rescue that had come to them just in time.

Four days later there was a gathering at Laramie. The general had come; the Fifth were there in camp, and a group of officers had assembled on the parade after the brief review of the command. The general turned from his staff, and singled out a captain of cavalry who stood close at hand.

"McCrea, I want to see that boy of yours. Where is he?"

An orderly sped away to the group of spectators and returned with a silent and embarrassed youth, who raised his hat respectfully, but said no word. The general stepped forward and held out both his hands.

"I'm proud to shake hands with you, young gentleman. I've heard all about you from the Fifth. You ought to go to West Point and be a cavalry officer."

"There's nothing I so much wish, general," stammered Ralph, with beaming eyes and burning cheeks.

"Then we'll telegraph his name to Washington this very day, gentlemen. I was asked to designate some young man for West Point who thoroughly deserved it, and is not this appointment well won?"

FROM "THE POINT" TO THE PLAINS.

CHAPTER I.

A CADET'S SISTER.

SHE was standing at the very end of the forward deck, and, with flushing cheeks and sparkling eyes, gazing eagerly upon the scene before her. Swiftly, smoothly rounding the rugged promontory on the right, the steamer was just turning into the highland "reach" at Fort Montgomery and heading straight away for the landings on the sunset shore. It was only mid-May, but the winter had been mild, the spring early, and now the heights on either side were clothed in raiment of the freshest, coolest green; the vines were climbing in luxuriant leaf all over the face of the rocky scarp that hemmed the swirling tide of the Hudson; the radiance of the evening sunshine bathed all the eastern shores in mellow light and left the dark slopes and deep gorges of the opposite range all the deeper and darker by contrast. A lively breeze had driven most of the passengers within doors as they sped through the broad waters of the Tappan Zee, but, once within the sheltering traverses of Dunderberg and the heights beyond, many of their number reappeared upon the promenade deck, and first among them was the bonnie little maid now clinging to the guard-rail at the very prow, and, heedless of fluttering skirt or fly-away curl, watching with all her soul in her bright blue eyes for the first glimpse of the haven where she would be. No eyes on earth look so eagerly for the grim, gray *façade* of the riding-hall or the domes and turrets of the library building as those of a girl who has spent the previous summer at West Point.

Utterly absorbed in her watch, she gave no heed to other passengers who presently took their station close at hand. One was a tall, dark-eyed, dark-haired young lady in simple and substantial travelling-dress. With her were two men in tweeds and Derby hats, and to these companions she constantly turned with questions as to prominent objects in the rich and varied landscape. It was evident that she was seeing for the first time sights that had been described to her time and again, for she was familiar with every name. One of the party was a man of over fifty years,—bronzed of face and gray of hair, but with erect carriage and piercing black eyes that spoke of vigor, energy, and probably of a life in the open air. It needed not the tri-colored button of the Loyal Legion in the lapel of his coat to tell that he was a soldier. Any one who chose to look—and there were not a few—could speedily have seen, too, that these were father and daughter.

The other man was still taller than the dark, wiry, slim-built soldier, but in years he was not more than twenty-eight or nine. His eyes, brows, hair, and the heavy moustache that drooped over his mouth were all of a dark, soft brown. His complexion was clear and ruddy; his frame powerful and athletic. Most of the time he stood a silent but attentive listener to the eager talk between the young lady and her father, but his kindly eyes rarely left her face; he was ready to respond when she turned to question him, and when he spoke it was with the unmistakable intonation of the South.

The deep, mellow tones of the bell were booming out their landing signal as the steamer shot into the shadow of a high, rocky cliff. Far aloft on the overhanging piazzas of a big hotel, fluttering handkerchiefs greeted the passengers on the decks below. Many eyes were turned thither in recognition of the salute, but not those of the young girl at the bow. One might, indeed, have declared her resentful of this intermediate stop. The instant the gray walls of the riding-school had come into view she had signalled, eagerly, with a wave of her hand, to a gentleman and lady seated in quiet conversation under the shelter of the deck. Presently the former, a burly, broad-shouldered man of forty or thereabouts, came sauntering forward and stood close behind her.

"Well, Nan! Most there, I see. Think you can hold on five minutes longer, or shall I toss you over and let you swim for it?"

For answer Miss Nan clasps a wooden pillar in her gray-gloved hands, and tilts excitedly on the toes of her tiny boots, never once relaxing her gaze on the dock a mile or more away up-stream.

"Just think of being so near Willy—and all of them—and not seeing one to speak to until after parade," she finally says.

"Simply inhuman!" answers her companion with commendable gravity, but with humorous twinkle about his eyes. "Is it worth all the long journey, and all the excitement in which your mother tells me you've been plunged for the past month?"

"Worth it, Uncle Jack?" and the blue eyes flash upon him indignantly. "Worth it? You wouldn't ask if you knew it all, as I do."

"Possibly not," says Uncle Jack, whimsically. "I haven't the advantage of being a girl with a brother and a baker's dozen of beaux in bell buttons and gray. I'm only an old fossil of a 'cit,' with a scamp of a nephew and that limited conception of the delights of West Point which one can derive from running up there every time that versatile youngster gets into a new scrape. You'll admit my opportunities have been frequent."

"It isn't Willy's fault, and you know it, Uncle Jack, though we all know how good you've been; but he's had more bad luck and—and—injustice than any cadet in the corps. Lots of his classmates told me so."

"Yes," says Uncle Jack, musingly. "That is what your blessed mother, yonder, wrote me when I went up last winter, the time Billy submitted that explanation to the commandant with its pleasing reference to the fox that had lost its tail—you doubtless recall the incident —and came within an ace of dismissal in consequence."

"I don't care!" interrupts Miss Nan, with flashing eyes. "Will had provocation enough to say much worse things: Jimmy Frazer wrote me so, and said the whole class was sticking up for him."

"I do not remember having had the honor of meeting Jimmy Frazer," remarks Uncle Jack, with an aggravating drawl that is peculiar to him. "Possibly he was one of the young gentlemen who didn't call, owing to some temporary impediment in the way of light prison——"

"Yes; and all because he took Will's part, as I believe," is the impetuous reply. "Oh! I'll be so thankful when they're out of it all."

"So will they, no doubt. 'Sticking up'—wasn't that Mr. Frazer's expression?—for Bill seems to have been an expensive luxury all round. Wonder if sticking up is something they continue when they get to their regiments? Billy has two or three weeks yet in which to ruin his chances of ever reaching one, and he has exhibited astonishing aptitude for tripping himself up thus far."

"Uncle Jack! How can you speak so of Willy, when he is so devoted to you? When he gets to his regiment there won't be any Lieutenant Lee to nag and worry him night and day. *He's* the cause of all the trouble."

"That so?" drawls Uncle Jack. "I didn't happen to meet Mr. Lee, either,—he was away on leave; but as Bill and your mother had some such views, I looked into things a bit. It appears to be a matter of record that my enterprising nephew had more demerit before the advent of Mr. Lee than since. As for 'extras' and confinements, his stock was always big enough to bear the market down to bottom prices."

The boat is once more under way, and a lull in the chat close at hand induces Uncle Jack to look about him. The younger of the two men lately standing with the dark-eyed girl has quietly withdrawn, and is now shouldering his way to a point out of ear-shot.

There he calmly turns and waits; his glance again resting upon her whose side he has so suddenly quitted. She has followed him with her eyes until he stops; then with heightened color resumes a low-toned chat with her father. Uncle Jack is a keen observer, and his next words are inaudible except to his niece.

"Nan, my child, I apprehend that remarks upon the characteristics of the officers at the Point had best be confined to the bosom of the family. We may be in their very midst."

She turns, flushing, and for the first time her blue eyes meet the dark ones of the older girl. Her cheeks redden still more, and she whirls about again.

"I can't help it, Uncle Jack," she murmurs. "I'd just like to tell them all what I think of Will's troubles."

"Oh! Candor is to be admired of all things," says Uncle Jack, airily. "Still it is just as well to observe the old adage, 'Be sure you're right,' etc. Now *I* own to being rather fond of Bill, despite all the worry he has given your mother, and all the bother he has been to me——"

"All the worry that others have given *him*, you ought to say, Uncle Jack."

"W-e-ll, har-d-ly. It didn't seem to me that the corps, as a rule, thought Billy the victim of persecution."

"They all tell *me* so, at least," is the indignant outburst.

"Do they, Nan? Well, of course, that settles it. Still, there were a few who reluctantly admitted having other views when I pressed them closely."

"Then they were no friends of Willy's, or mine either!"

"Now, do you know, I thought just the other way? I thought one of them, especially, a very stanch friend of Billy's and yours, too, Nan, but Billy seems to consider advisers in the light of adversaries."

A moment's pause. Then, with cheeks still red, and plucking at the rope netting with nervous fingers, Miss Nan essays a tentative. Her eyes are downcast as she asks,—

"I suppose you mean Mr. Stanley?"

"The very man, Nanette; very much of a man to my thinking."

The bronzed soldier standing near cannot but have heard the name and the words. His face takes on a glow and the black eyes kindle.

"Mr. Stanley would not say to *me* that Willy is to blame," pouts the maiden, and her little foot is beating impatiently tattoo on the deck.

"Neither would I—just now—if I were Mr. Stanley; but all the same, he decidedly opposed the view that Mr. Lee was 'down on Billy,' as your mother seems to think."

"That's because Mr. Lee is tactical officer commanding the company, and Mr. Stanley is cadet captain. Oh! I will take him to task if he has been— been——"

But she does not finish. She has turned quickly in speaking, her hand clutching a little knot of bell buttons hanging by a chain at the front of her dress. She has turned just in time to catch a warning glance in Uncle Jack's twinkling eyes, and to see a grim smile lurking under the gray moustache of the gentleman with the Loyal Legion button who is leading away the tall young lady with the dark hair. In another moment they have rejoined the third member of their party,—he who first withdrew,—and it is evident that something has happened which gives them all much amusement. They are chatting eagerly together, laughing not a little, although the laughter, like their words, is entirely inaudible to Miss Nan. But she feels a twinge of indignation when the tall girl turns and looks directly at her. There is nothing unkindly in the glance. There even is merriment in the dark, handsome eyes and lurking among the dimples around that beautiful mouth. Why did those eyes —so heavily fringed, so thickly shaded—seem to her familiar as old friends? Nan could have vowed she had somewhere met that girl before, and now that girl was laughing at her. Not rudely, not aggressively, to be sure,—she had turned away again the instant she saw that the little maiden's eyes were upon her,—but all the same, said Nan to herself, she *was* laughing. They were all laughing, and it must have been because of her outspoken defence of Brother Will and equally outspoken defiance of his persecutors. What made it worse was that Uncle Jack was laughing too.

"Do you know who they are?" she demands, indignantly.

"Not I, Nan," responds Uncle Jack. "Never saw them before in my life, but I warrant we see them again, and at the Point, too. Come, child. There's our bell, and we must start for the gangway. Your mother is hailing us now. Never mind this time, little woman," he continues, kindly, as he notes the cloud on her brow. "I don't think any harm has been done, but it is just as well not to be impetuous in public speech. Ah! I thought so. They are to get off here with us."

Three minutes more and a little stream of passengers flows out upon the broad government dock, and, as luck would have it, Uncle Jack and his charges are just behind the trio in which, by this time, Miss Nan is deeply, if not painfully, interested. A soldier in the undress uniform of a corporal of artillery hastens forward and, saluting, stretches forth his hand to take the satchel carried by the tall man with the brown moustache.

"The lieutenant's carriage is at the gate," he says, whereat Uncle Jack, who is conducting her mother just in front, looks back over his shoulder and nods compassionately at Nan.

"Has any despatch been sent down to meet Colonel Stanley?" she hears the tall man inquire, and this time Uncle Jack's backward glance is a combination of mischief and concern.

"Nothing, sir, and the adjutant's orderly is here now. This is all he brought down," and the corporal hands to the inquirer a note, the superscription of which the young officer quickly scans; then turns and, while his soft brown eyes light with kindly interest and he bares his shapely head, accosts the lady on Uncle Jack's arm,—

"Pardon me, madam. This note must be for you. Mrs. McKay, is it not?"

And as her mother smiles her thanks and the others

turn away, Nan's eager eyes catch sight of Will's well-known writing. Mrs. McKay rapidly reads it as Uncle Jack is bestowing bags and bundles in the omnibus and feeing the acceptive porter, who now rushes back to the boat in the nick of time.

"Awful sorry I can't get up to the hotel to see you," says the note, dolorously, but by no means unexpectedly. "I'm in confinement and can't get a permit. Come to the officer-in-charge's office right after supper, and he'll let me see you there awhile. Stanley's officer of the day, and he'll be there to show the way. In haste, WILL."

"Now *isn't* that poor Willy's luck every time!" exclaims Miss Nan, her blue eyes threatening to fill with tears. "I *do* think they might let him off the day we get here."

"Unquestionably," answers Uncle Jack, with great gravity, as he assists the ladies into the yellow omnibus. "You duly notified the superintendent of your impending arrival, I suppose?"

Mrs. McKay smiles quietly. Hers is a sweet and gentle face, lined with many a trace of care and anxiety. Her brother's whimsical ways are old acquaintances, and she knows how to treat them; but Nan is young, impulsive, and easily teased. She flares up instantly.

"Of course we *didn't*, Uncle Jack; how utterly absurd it would sound! But Willy knew we were coming, and *he* must have told him when he asked for his permit, and it does seem too hard that he was refused."

"Heartless in the last degree," says Uncle Jack, sympathetically, but with the same suggestive drawl. "Yonder go the father and sister of the young gentleman whom you announced your intention to castigate because he didn't agree that Billy was being abused, Nan. You will have a chance this very evening, won't you? He's officer of the day, according to Billy's note, and can't escape. You'll have wound up the whole family by tattoo. Quite a good day's work. Billy's opposers will do well to take warning and keep out of the way hereafter," he continues, teasingly. "Oh—ah —*corporal!*" he calls, "who was the young officer who just drove off in the carriage with the lady and gentleman?"

"That was Lieutenant Lee, sir."

Uncle Jack turns and contemplates his niece with an expression of the liveliest admiration. "'Pon my word, Miss Nan, you are a most comprehensive young person. You've indeed let no guilty man escape."

CHAPTER II.

A CADET SCAPEGRACE.

THE evening that opened so clear and sunshiny has clouded rapidly over. Even as the four gray companies come "trotting" in from parade, and, with the ease of long habit, quickly forming line in the barrack area, some heavy rain-drops begin to fall; the drum-major has hurried his band away; the crowd of spectators, unusually large for so early in the season, scatters for shelter; umbrellas pop up here and there under the beautiful trees along the western roadway; the adjutant rushes through "delinquency list" in a style distinguishable only to his stolid, silent audience standing immovably before him,—a long perspective of gray uniforms and glistening white belts. The fateful book is closed with a snap, and the echoing walls ring to the quick commands of the first sergeants, at which the bayonets are struck from the rifle-barrels, and the long line bursts into a living torrent sweeping into the hallways to escape the coming shower.

When the battalion reappears, a few moments later, every man is in his overcoat, and here and there little knots of upper classmen gather, and there is eager and excited talk.

A soldierly, dark-eyed young fellow, with the red sash of the officer of the day over his shoulder, comes briskly out of the hall of the fourth division. The chevrons of a cadet captain are glistening on his arm, and he alone has not donned the gray overcoat, although he has discarded the plumed shako in deference to the coming storm; yet he hardly seems to notice the downpour of the rain; his face is grave and his lips set and compressed as he rapidly makes his way through the groups awaiting the signal to "fall in" for supper.

"Stanley! O Stanley!" is the hail from a knot of classmates, and he halts and looks about as two or three of the party hasten after him.

"What does Billy say about it?" is the eager inquiry.

"Nothing—new."

"Well, that report as good as finds him on demerit, doesn't it?"

"The next thing to it; though he has been as close to the brink before."

"But—great Scott! He has two weeks yet to run; and Billy McKay can no more live two weeks without demerit than Patsy, here, without 'spooning.'"

Mr. Stanley's eyes look tired as he glances up from under the visor of his forage cap. He is not as tall by half a head as the young soldiers by whom he is surrounded.

"We were talking of his chances at dinner-time," he says, gravely. "Billy never mentioned this break of his yesterday, and was surprised to hear the report read out to-night. I believe he had forgotten the whole thing."

"Who 'skinned' him?—Lee? He was there."

"I don't know; McKay says so, but there were several officers over there at the time. It is a report he cannot get off, and it comes at a most unlucky moment."

With this remark Mr. Stanley turns away and goes striding through the crowded area towards the guard-house. Another moment and there is sudden drum-beat; the gray overcoats leap into ranks; the subject of the recent discussion—a jaunty young fellow with laughing blue eyes—comes tearing out of the fourth division just in time to avoid a "late," and the clamor of tenscore voices gives place to silence broken only by the rapid calling of the rolls and the prompt "here" —"here," in response.

If ever there was a pet in the corps of cadets he lived in the person of Billy McKay. Bright as one of his own buttons; jovial, generous, impulsive; he had only one enemy in the battalion,—and that one, as he had been frequently told, was himself. This, however, was a matter which he could not at all be induced to believe. Of the Academic Board in general, of his instructors in large measure, but of the four or five ill-starred soldiers known as "tactical officers" in particular, Mr. McKay entertained very decided and most unflattering opinions. He had won his cadetship through rigid competitive examination against all comers; he was a natural mathematician of whom a professor had said that he "*could* stand in the fives and *wouldn't* stand in the forties;" years of his boyhood spent in France had made him master of the colloquial forms of the court language of Europe, yet a dozen classmates who had never seen a French verb before their admission stood above him at the end of the first term. He had gone to the first section like a rocket and settled to the bottom of it like a stick. No subject in the course was really hard to him, his natural aptitude enabling him to triumph over the toughest problems. Yet he hated work, and would often face about with an empty black-board and take a zero and a report for neglect of studies that half an hour's application would have rendered impossible. Classmates who saw impending danger would frequently make stolen visits to his room towards the close of the term and profess to be baffled by the lesson for the morrow, and Billy would promptly knock the ashes out of the pipe he was smoking contrary to regulations and lay aside the guitar on which he had been softly strumming—also contrary to regulations; would pick up the neglected calculus or mechanics; get interested in the work of explanation, and end by having learned the lesson in spite of himself. This was too good a joke to be kept a secret, and by the time the last year came Billy had found it all out and refused to be longer hoodwinked.

There was never the faintest danger of his being found deficient in studies, but there was ever the glaring prospect of his being discharged "on demerit." Mr. McKay and the regulations of the United States Military Academy had been at loggerheads from the start.

And yet, frank, jolly, and generous as he was in all intercourse with his comrades, there was never a time when this young gentleman could be brought to see that in such matters he was the arbiter of his own destiny. Like the Irishman whose first announcement on setting foot on American soil was that he was "agin the government," Billy McKay believed that regulations were made only to oppress; that the men who drafted such a code were idiots, and that those whose duty it became to enforce it were simply spies and tyrants, resistance to whom was innate virtue. He was forever ignoring or violating some written or unwritten law of the Academy; was frequently being caught in the act, and was invariably ready to attribute the resultant report to ill luck which pursued no one else, or to a deliberate persecution which followed him forever. Every six months he had been on the verge of dismissal, and now, a fortnight from the final examination, with a margin of only six demerit to run on, Mr. Billy McKay had just been read out in the daily list of culprits or victims as "Shouting from window of barracks to cadets in area during study hours,— three forty-five and four P.M."

There was absolutely no excuse for this performance. The regulations enjoined silence and order in barracks during "call to quarters." It had been raining a little, and he was in hopes there would be no battalion drill, in which event he would venture on throwing off his uniform and spreading himself out on his bed with a pipe and a novel,—two things he dearly loved. Ten minutes would have decided the question legitimately for him, but, being of impatient temperament, he could not wait, and, catching sight of the adjutant and the senior captain coming from the guard-house, Mr. McKay sung out in tones familiar to every man within ear-shot,—

"Hi, Jim! Is it battalion drill?"

The adjutant glanced quickly up,—a warning glance as he could have seen,—merely shook his head, and went rapidly on, while his comrade, the cadet first captain, clinched his fist at the window and growled between his set teeth, "Be quiet, you idiot!"

But poor Billy persisted. Louder yet he called,—

"Well—say—Jimmy! Come up here after four o'clock. I'll be in confinement, and can't come out. Want to see you."

And the windows over at the office of the commandant being wide open, and that official being seated there in consultation with three or four of his assistants, and as Mr. McKay's voice was as well known to them as to the corps, there was no alternative. The colonel himself "confounded" the young scamp for his recklessness, and directed a report to be entered against him.

And now, as Mr. Stanley is betaking himself to his post at the guard-house, his heart is heavy within him because of this new load on his comrade's shoulders.

"How on earth could you have been so careless, Billy?" he had asked him as McKay, fuming and indignant, was throwing off his accoutrements in his room on the second floor.

"How'd I know anybody was over there?" was the boyish reply. "It's just a skin on suspicion anyhow. Lee couldn't have seen me, nor could anybody else. I stood way back by the clothes-press."

"There's no suspicion about it, Billy. There isn't a man that walks the area that doesn't know your voice as well as he does Jim Pennock's. Confound it! You'll get over the limit yet, man, and break your— your mother's heart."

"Oh, come now, Stan! You've been nagging me ever since last camp. Why 'n thunder can't you see I'm doing my best? Other men don't row me as you do, or stand up for the 'tacks.' I tell you that fellow Lee never loses a chance of skinning me: he *takes* chances, by gad, and I'll make his eyes pop out of his head when he reads what I've got to say about it."

"You're too hot for reason now, McKay," said Stanley, sadly. "Step out or you'll get a late for supper. I'll see you after awhile. I gave that note to the orderly, by the way, and he said he'd take it down to the dock himself."

"Mother and Nan will probably come to the guardhouse right after supper. Look out for them for me, will you, Stan, until old Snipes gets there and sends for me?"

And as Mr. Stanley shut the door instantly and went clattering down the iron stairs, Mr. McKay caught no sign on his face of the sudden flutter beneath that snugly-buttoned coat.

It was noticed by more than one of the little coterie at his own table that the officer of the day hurried through his supper and left the mess-hall long before the command for the first company to rise. It was a matter well known to every member of the graduating class that, almost from the day of her arrival during the encampment of the previous summer, Phil Stanley had been a devoted admirer of Miss Nannie McKay. It was not at all to be wondered at.

Without being what is called an ideal beauty, there was a fascination about this winsome little maid which few could resist. She had all her brother's impulsiveness, all his enthusiasm, and, it may be safely asserted, all his abiding faith in the sacred and unimpeachable character of cadet friendships. If she possessed a little streak of romance that was not discernible in him, she managed to keep it well in the background; and though she had her favorites in the corps, she was so frank and cordial and joyous in her manner to all that it was impossible to say which one, if any, she regarded in the light of a lover. Whatever comfort her gentle mother may have derived from this state of affairs, it was "hard lines on Stanley," as his classmates put it, for there could be little doubt that the captain of the color company was a sorely-smitten man.

He was not what is commonly called a "popular man" in the corps. The son of a cavalry officer, reared on the wide frontier and educated only imperfectly, he had not been able to enter the Academy until nearly twenty years of age, and nothing but indomitable will and diligence had carried him through the difficulties of the first half of the course. It was not until the middle of the third year that the chevrons of a sergeant were awarded him, and even then the battalion was taken by surprise. There was no surprise a few months later, however, when he was promoted over a score of classmates and made captain of his company. It was an open secret that the commandant had said that if he had it all to do over again, Mr. Stanley would be made "first captain,"—a rumor that big John Burton, the actual incumbent of that office, did not at all fancy. Stanley was "square" and impartial. His company was in admirable discipline, though many of his classmates growled and wished he were not "so confoundedly military." The second classmen, always the most critical judges of the qualifications of their seniors, conceded that he was more soldierly than any man of his year, but were unanimous in the opinion that he should show more deference to men of their standing in the corps. The "yearlings" swore by him in any discussion as to the relative merits of the four captains; but with equal energy swore at him when contemplating that fateful volume known as "the skin book." The fourth classmen—the "plebes"—simply worshipped the ground he trod on, and as between General Sherman and Philip Stanley, it is safe to say these youngsters would have determined on the latter as the more suitable candidate for the office of general-in-chief. Of course they admired the adjutant,—the plebes always do that,—and not infrequently to the exclusion of the other cadet officers; but there was something grand, to them, about this dark-eyed, dark-faced, dignified captain who never stooped to trifle with them; was always so precise and courteous, and yet so immeasurably distant. They were ten times more afraid of him than they had been of Lieutenant Rolfe, who was their "tack" during camp, or of the great, handsome, kindly-voiced dragoon who succeeded him, Lieutenant Lee, of the —th Cavalry. They approved of this latter gentleman because he belonged to the regiment of which Mr. Stanley's father was lieutenant-colonel, and to which it was understood Mr. Stanley was to be assigned on his graduation. What they could not at all understand was that, once graduated, Mr. Stanley could step down from his high position in the battalion of cadets and become a mere file-closer. Yes. Stanley was too strict and soldierly to command that decidedly ephemeral tribute known as "popularity," but no man in the corps of cadets was more thoroughly respected. If there were flaws in the armor of his personal character they were not such as to be vigorously prodded by his comrades. He had firm friends,—devoted friends, who grew to honor and trust him more with every year; but, strong though they knew him to be, he had found his conqueror. There was a story in the first class that in Stanley's old leather writing-case was a sort of secret compartment, and in this compartment was treasured "a knot of ribbon blue" that had been worn last summer close under the dimpled white chin of pretty Nannie McKay.

And now on this moist May evening as he hastens back to barracks, Mr. Stanley spies a little group standing in front of the guard-house. Lieutenant Lee is there,—in his uniform now,—and with him are the tall girl in the simple travelling-dress, and the trim, wiry, gray-moustached soldier whom we saw on the boat. The rain is falling steadily, which accounts for and possibly excuses Mr. Lee's retention of the young lady's arm in his as he holds the umbrella over both ; but the colonel no sooner catches sight of the officer of the day than his own umbrella is cast aside, and with light, eager, buoyant steps, father and son hasten to meet each other. In an instant their hands are clasped,—both hands,— and through moistening eyes the veteran of years of service and the boy in whom his hopes are centred gaze into each other's faces.

" Phil,—my son !"

" Father !"

No other words. It is the first meeting in two long years. The area is deserted save by the smiling pair watching from under the dripping umbrella with eyes nearly as moist as the skies. There is no one to comment or to scoff. In the father's heart, mingling with the deep joy at this reunion with his son, there wells up sudden, irrepressible sorrow. " Ah, God !" he thinks. " Could his mother but have lived to see him now !" Perhaps Philip reads it all in the strong yet tremulous clasp of those sinewy brown hands, but for the moment neither speaks again. There are some joys so deep, some heart longings so overpowering, that many a man is forced to silence, or to a levity of manner which is utterly repugnant to him, in the effort to conceal from the world the tumult of emotion that so nearly makes him weep. Who that has read that inimitable page will ever forget the meeting of that genial sire and gallant son in the grimy old railway car filled with the wounded from Antietam, in Doctor Holmes's "My Search for the Captain?"

When Phil Stanley, still clinging to his father's hand, turns to greet his sister and her handsome escort, he is suddenly aware of another group that has entered the area. Two ladies, marshalled by his classmate, Mr. Pennock, are almost at his side, and one of them is the blue-eyed girl he loves.

CHAPTER III.

"AMANTIUM IRÆ."

LOVELY as is West Point in May, it is hardly the best time for a visit there if one's object be to see the cadets. From early morn until late at night every hour is taken up with duties, academic or military. Mothers, sisters, and sweethearts, whose eyes so eagerly follow the evolutions of the gray ranks, can only hope for a few words between drill and dress parade, or else in the shortest half-hour in all the world,—that which intervenes 'twixt supper and evening " call to quarters." That Miss Nannie McKay should make frequent and unfavorable comment on this state of affairs goes without saying; yet, had she been enabled to see her beloved brother but once a month and her cadet friends at intervals almost as rare, that incomprehensible young damsel would have preferred the Point to any other place in the world.

It was now ten days since her arrival, and she had had perhaps three chats with Willy, who, luckily for him, though he could not realize it, was spending most of his time "confined to quarters," and consequently out of much of the temptation he would otherwise have been in. Mrs. McKay had been able to see very little more of the young man, but she had the prayerful consolation that if he could only be kept out of mischief a few days longer he would then be through with it all, out of danger of dismissal, actually graduated, and once more her own boy to monopolize as she chose.

It takes most mothers a long, long time to become reconciled to the complete usurpation of all their former rights by this new parent whom their boys are bound to serve,—this anything but *Alma* Mater,—the war school of the nation. As for Miss Nan, though she made it a point to declaim vigorously at the fates that prevented her seeing more of her brother, it was wonderful how well she looked and in what blithe spirits she spent her days. Regularly as the sun came around, before guard-mount in the morning and right after supper in the evening, she was sure to be on the south piazza of the old hotel, and when presently the cadet uniforms began to appear at the hedge, she, and others, would go tripping lightly down the path to meet the wearers, and then would follow the half-hour's walk and chat in which she found such infinite delight. So, too, could Mr. Stanley, had he been able to appear as her escort on all occasions; but despite his strong personal inclination and effort, this was by no means the case. The little lady was singularly impartial in the distribution of her time, and only by being first applicant had he secured to himself the one long afternoon that had yet been vouchsafed them,—the cadet half-holiday of Saturday.

But if Miss Nan found time hanging heavily on her hands at other hours of the day, there was one young lady at the hotel who did not,—a young lady whom, by this time, she regarded with constantly deepening interest,—Miriam Stanley.

Other girls, younger girls, who had found their ideals in the cadet gray, were compelled to spend hours of the twenty-four in waiting for the too brief *half*-hour in which it was possible to meet them; but Miss Stanley was very differently situated. It was her first visit to the Point. She met, and was glad to meet, all Philip's friends and comrades; but it was plainly to be seen, said all the girls at Craney's, that between her and the tall cavalry officer whom they best knew through cadet descriptions, there existed what they termed an "understanding," if not an engagement. Every day, when not prevented by duties, Mr. Lee would come stalking up from barracks, and presently away they would stroll together,—a singularly handsome pair, as every one admitted. One morning soon after the Stanleys' arrival he appeared in saddle on his stylish bay, accompanied by an orderly leading another horse, side-saddled; and then, as by common impulse, all the girls promenading the piazzas, as was their wont, with arms entwining each other's waists, came flocking about the south steps. When Miss Stanley appeared in her riding-habit and was quickly swung up into saddle by her cavalier, and then, with a bright nod and smile for the entire group, she gathered the reins in her practised hand and rode briskly away, the sentiments of the fair spectators were best expressed, perhaps, in the remark of Miss McKay,—

"What a shame it is that the cadets can't ride! I mean can't ride—*that* way," she explained, with suggestive nod of her curly head towards the pair just trotting out upon the road around the Plain. "They ride—lots of them—better than most of the officers."

"Mr. Stanley for instance," suggests a mischievous little minx with hazel eyes and laughter-loving mouth.

"Yes, Mr. Stanley, or Mr. Pennock, or Mr. Burton, or a dozen others I could name, not excepting my brother," answers Miss Nan, stoutly, although those readily flushing cheeks of hers promptly throw out their signals of perturbation. "Fancy Mr. Lee vaulting over his horse at the gallop as they do."

"And yet Mr. Lee has taught them so much more than other instructors. Several cadets have told me so. He always does, first, everything he requires them to do; so he must be able to make that vault."

"Will doesn't say so by any means," retorts Nannie, with something very like a pout; and as Will is a prime favorite with the entire party and the centre of a wide circle of interest, sympathy, and anxiety in those girlish hearts, their loyalty is proof against opinions that may not coincide with his. "Miss Mischief" reads temporary defeat in the circle of bright faces and is stung to new effort,—

"Well! there are cadets whose opinions you value quite as much as you do your brother's, Nannie, and they have told me."

"Who?" challenges Miss Nan, yet with averted face. Thrice of late she has disagreed with Mr. Stanley about Willy's troubles; has said things to him which she wishes she had left unsaid; and for two days now he has not sought her side as heretofore, though she knows he has been at the hotel to see his sister, and a little bird has told her he had a long talk with this same hazel-eyed girl. She wants to know more about it,—yet does not want to ask.

"Phil Stanley, for one," is the not unexpected answer.

Somebody who appears to know all about it has written that when a girl is beginning to feel deep interest in a man she will say things decidedly detrimental to his character solely for the purpose of having them denied and for the pleasure of hearing him defended. Is it this that prompts Miss McKay to retort?—

"Mr. Stanley cares too little what his classmates think, and too much of what Mr. Lee may say or do."

"Mr. Stanley isn't the only one who thinks a deal of Lieutenant Lee," is the spirited answer. "Mr. Burton says he is the most popular tactical officer here, and many a cadet—good friends of your brother's, Nannie—has said the same thing. You don't like him because Will doesn't."

"I wouldn't like or respect any officer who reports cadets on suspicion," is the stout reply. "If he did that to any one else I would despise it as much as I do because Willy is the victim."

The discussion is waxing hot. "Miss Mischief's" blood is up. She likes Phil Stanley; she likes Mr.

Lee; she has hosts of friends in the corps, and she is just as loyal and quite as pronounced in her views as her little adversary. They are fond of each other, too, and were great chums all through the previous summer; but there is danger of a quarrel to-day.

"I don't think you are just in that matter at all, Nannie. I have heard cadets say that if they had been in Mr. Lee's place or on officer-of-the-day duty they would have had to give Will that report you take so much to heart. Everybody knows his voice. Half the corps heard him call out to Mr. Pennock."

"I don't believe a single cadet who's a friend of Will's would say such a thing," bursts in Miss Nan, her eyes blazing.

"He is a friend, and a warm friend, too."

"You said there were several, Kitty, and I don't believe it possible."

"Well. There were two or three. If you don't believe it, you can ask Mr. Stanley. *He* said it, and the others agreed.

Fancy the mood in which she meets him this particular evening, when his card was brought to her door. Twice has "Miss Mischief" essayed to enter the room and "make up." Conscience has been telling her savagely that in the impulse and sting of the moment she has given an unfair coloring to the whole matter. Mr. Stanley had volunteered no such remark as that she so vehemently quoted. Asked point blank whether he considered as given "on suspicion" the report which Mrs. McKay and Nannie so resented, he replied that he did not; and, when further pressed, he said that Will alone was blamable in the matter: Mr.

Lee had no alternative, if it was Mr. Lee who gave the report, and any other officer would have been compelled to do the same. All this "Miss Mischief" would gladly have explained to Nannie could she have gained admission, but the latter "had a splitting headache," and begged to be excused.

It has been such a lovely afternoon. The halls were filled with cadets "on permit," when she came out from the dining-room, but nothing but ill-luck seemed to attend her. The young gentleman who had invited her to walk to Fort Putnam, most provokingly twisted an ankle at cavalry drill that very morning, and was sent to hospital. *Now*, if Mr. Stanley were all devotion, he would promptly tender his services as substitute. Then she could take him to task and punish him for his disloyalty to Will. But Mr. Stanley was not to be seen: "Gone off with another girl," was the announcement made to her by Mr. Werrick, a youth who dearly loved a joke, and who saw no need of explaining that the other girl was his own sister. Sorely disappointed, yet hardly knowing why, she accepted her mother's invitation to go with her to the barracks where Will was promenading the area on what Mr. Werrick called "one of his perennial punishment tours." She went, of course; but the distant sight of poor Will, duly equipped as a sentry, dismally tramping up and down the asphalt, added fuel to the inward fire that consumed her. The mother's heart, too, yearned over her boy,—a victim to cruel regulations and crueler task-masters. "What was the use of the government's enticing young men away from their comfortable homes," Mrs. McKay had once indignantly written, "unless it could make them happy?" It was a question the "tactical department" could not answer, but it thought volumes.

But now evening had come, and with it Mr. Stanley's card. Nan's heart gave a bound, but she went downstairs with due deliberation. She had his card in her hand as she reached the hall, and was twisting it in her fingers. Yes. There he stood on the north piazza, Pennock with him, and one or two others of the graduating class. They were chatting laughingly with Miss Stanley, "Miss Mischief," a bevy of girls, and a matron or two, but she knew well his eyes would be on watch for her. They were. He saw her instantly; bowed, smiled, but, to her surprise, continued his conversation with a lady seated near the door. What could it mean? Irresolute she stood there a moment, waiting for him to come forward; but though she saw that twice his eyes sought hers, he was still bending courteously and listening to the voluble words of the somewhat elderly dame who claimed his attention. Nan began to rebel against that woman from the bottom of her heart. What was she to do? Here was his card. In response she had come down to receive him. She meant to be very cool from the first moment; to provoke him to inquiry as to the cause of such unusual conduct, and then to upbraid him for his disloyalty to her brother. She certainly meant that he should feel the weight of her displeasure; but then—then—after he had been made to suffer, if he was properly contrite, and said so, and looked it, and begged to be forgiven, why then, perhaps she might be brought to condone it in a measure and be good friends again. It was clearly his duty, however, to come and greet her, not hers to go to the laughing group. The old lady was the only one among them whom she did not know,—a new arrival. Just then Miss Stanley looked round, saw her, and signalled smilingly to her to come and join them. Slowly she walked towards the little party, still twirling the card in her taper fingers.

"Looking for anybody, Nan?" blithely hails " Miss Mischief." "Who is it? I see you have his card."

For once Nannie's voice fails her, and she knows not what to say. Before she can frame an answer there is a rustle of skirts and a light foot-fall behind her, and she hears the voice of a girl whom she never has liked one bit.

"Oh! You're here, are you, Mr. Stanley! Why, I've been waiting at least a quarter of an hour. Did you send up your card?"

"I did; full ten minutes ago. Was it not brought to your room?"

"No, indeed! I've been sitting there writing, and only came down because I had promised Mr. Fearn that he should have ten minutes, and it is nearly his time now. Where do you suppose they could have sent it?"

Poor little Nan! It has been a hard day for her, but this is just too much. She turns quickly, and, hardly knowing whither she goes, dodges past the party of cadets and girls now blocking the stairway and preventing flight to her room, hurries out the south door and around to the west piazza, and there, leaning against a pillar, is striving to hide her blazing cheeks,— all in less than a minute.

Stanley sees through the entire situation with the quick intuition of a lover. She has not treated him kindly of late. She has been capricious and unjust on several occasions, but there is no time to think of that now. She is in distress, and that is more than enough for him.

"Here comes Mr. Fearn himself to claim his walk, so I will go and find out about the card," he says, and blesses that little rat of a bell-boy as he hastens away.

Out on the piazza he finds her alone, yet with half a dozen people hovering nigh. The hush of twilight is over the beautiful old Point. The moist breath of the coming night, cool and sweet, floats down upon them from the deep gorges on the rugged flank of Cro' Nest, and rises from the thickly lacing branches of the cedars on the river-bank below. A flawless mirror in its grand and reflected framework of cliff and crag and beetling precipice, the Hudson stretches away northward unruffled by the faintest cat's-paw of a breeze. Far beyond the huge black battlements of Storm King and the purpled scaur of Breakneck the night lights of the distant city are twinkling through the gathering darkness, and tiny dots of silvery flame down in the cool depths beneath them reflect the faint glimmer from the cloudless heaven where—

"The sentinel stars set their watch in the sky."

The hush of the sacred hour has fallen on every lip save those of the merry party in the hall, where laugh and chatter and flaring gas-light bid defiance to influences such as hold their sway over souls brought face to face with Nature in this, her loveliest haunt on earth.

Phil Stanley's heart is throbbing as he steps quickly to her side. Well, indeed, she knows his foot-fall; knows he is coming; almost knows *why* he comes. She is burning with a sense of humiliation, wounded pride, maidenly wrath, and displeasure. All day long everything has gone agley. Could she but flee to her room and hide her flaming cheeks and cry her heart out, it would be relief inexpressible, but her retreat is cut off. She cannot escape. She cannot face those keen-eyed watchers in the hall-ways. Oh! it is almost maddening that she should have been so—so fooled! Every one must know she came down to meet Phil Stanley when his card was meant for another girl,— that girl of all others! All aflame with indignation as she is, she yet means to freeze him if she can only control herself.

"Miss Nannie," he murmurs, quick and low, "I see that a blunder has been made, but I don't believe the others saw it. Give me just a few minutes. Come down the walk with me. I cannot talk with you here —now, and there is so much I want to say." He bends over her pleadingly, but her eyes are fixed far away up the dark wooded valley beyond the white shafts of the cemetery, gleaming in the first beams of the rising moon. She makes no reply for a moment. She does not withdraw them when finally she answers, impressively,—

"Thank you, Mr. Stanley, but I must be excused from interfering with your engagements."

"There is no engagement now," he promptly replies;

"and I greatly want to speak with you. Have you been quite kind to me of late? Have I not a right to know what has brought about the change?"

"You do not seem to have sought opportunity to inquire,"—very cool and dignified now.

"Pardon me. Three times this week I have asked for a walk, and you have had previous engagements."

She has torn to bits and thrown away the card that was in her hand. Now she is tugging at the bunch of bell buttons, each graven with the monogram of some cadet friend, that hangs as usual by its tiny golden chain. She wants to say that he has found speedy consolation in the society of "that other girl" of whom Mr. Werrick spoke, but not for the world would she seem jealous.

"You could have seen me this afternoon, had there been any matters you wished explained," she says. "I presume you were more agreeably occupied."

"I find no delight in formal visits," he answers, quietly; "but my sister wished to return calls and asked me to show her about the post."

Then it was his sister. Not "that other girl!" Still she must not let him see it makes her glad. She needs a pretext for her wrath. She must make him feel it in some way. This is not at all in accordance with the mental private rehearsals she has been having. There is still that direful matter of Will's report for "shouting from window of barracks," and "Miss Mischief's" equally direful report of Mr. Stanley's remarks thereon.

"I thought you were a loyal friend of Willy's," she says, turning suddenly upon him.

"I was—and am," he answers simply.

"And yet I'm told you said it was all his own fault, and that you yourself would have given him the report that so nearly 'found him on demerit.' A report on suspicion, too," she adds, with scorn in her tone.

Mr. Stanley is silent a moment.

"You have heard a very unfair account of my words," he says at last. "I have volunteered no opinions on the subject. In answer to direct question I have said that it was not justifiable to call that a report on suspicion."

"But you said you would have given it yourself."

"I said that, as officer of the day, I would have been compelled to do so. I could not have signed my certificate otherwise."

She turns away in speechless indignation. What makes it all well-nigh intolerable is that he is by no means on the defensive. He is patient, gentle, but decidedly superior. Not at all what she wanted. Not at all eager to explain, argue, or implore. Not at all the tearful penitent she has pictured in her plans. She must bring him to a realizing sense of the enormity of his conduct. Disloyalty to Will is treason to her.

"And yet—you say you have kept, and that you value, that knot of blue ribbon that I gave you—or that you took—last summer. I did not suppose that you would so soon prove to be—no friend to Willy, or——"

"Or what, Miss Nannie?" he asks. His face is growing white, but he controls the tremor in his voice. She does not see. Her eyes are downcast and her face averted now, but she goes on desperately.

"Well, never mind *that* now; but it seems to me that such friendship is—simply worthless."

She has taken the plunge and said her say, but the last words are spoken with sinking inflection, followed instantly by a sinking heart. He makes no answer whatever. She dares not look up into his face to see the effect of her stab. He stands there silent only an instant; then raises his cap, turns, and leaves her.

Sunday comes and goes without a sight of him except in the line of officers at parade. That night she goes early to her room, and on the bureau finds a little box securely tied, sealed, and addressed to her in his well-known hand. It contains a note and some soft object carefully wrapped in tissue-paper. The note is brief enough:

"It is not easy to part with this, for it is all I have that was yours to give, but even this must be returned to you after what you said last night.

"Miss Nannie, you may some time think more highly of my friendship for your brother than you do now, and then, perhaps, will realize that you were very unjust. Should that time come I shall be glad to have this again."

It was hardly necessary to open the little packet as she did. She knew well enough it could contain only that

"Knot of ribbon blue."

CHAPTER IV.

"THE WOMAN TEMPTED ME."

JUNE is here. The examinations are in full blast. The Point is thronged with visitors and every hostelrie in the neighborhood has opened wide its doors to accommodate the swarms of people interested in the graduating exercises and eager for the graduating ball. Pretty girls there are in force, and at Craney's they are living three and four in a room; the joy of being really there on the Point, near the cadets, aroused by the morning gun and shrill piping of the reveille, saluted hourly by the notes of the bugle, enabled to see the gray uniforms half a dozen times a day and to actually speak or walk with the wearers half an hour out of twenty-four whole ones, being apparent compensation for any crowding or discomfort. Indeed, crowded as they are, the girls at Craney's are objects of boundless envy to those whom the Fates have consigned to the resorts down around the picturesque but distant "Falls." There is a little coterie at "Hawkshurst" that is fiercely jealous of the sisterhood in the favored nook at the north edge of the Plain, and one of their number, who is believed to have completely subjugated that universal favorite, Cadet McKay, has been heard to say that she thought it an outrage that they had to come home so early in the evening and mope away the time without a single cadet, when up there at Craney's the halls and piazzas were full of gray-coats and bell buttons every night until tattoo.

A very brilliant and pretty girl she is, too, and neither Mrs. McKay nor Nannie can wonder at it that Will's few leisure moments are monopolized. "You are going to have me all to yourself next week, little mother," he laughingly explains; "and goodness knows when I'm going to see Miss Waring again." And though neither mother nor sister is at all satisfied with the state of affairs, both are too unselfish to interpose. How many an hour have mothers and, sometimes, sisters waited in loneliness at the old hotel for boys whom some other fellow's sister was holding in silken fetters somewhere down in shady "Flirtation!"

It was with relief inexpressible that Mrs. McKay and Uncle Jack had hailed the coming of the 1st of June. With a margin of only two demerits Will had safely weathered the reefs and was practically safe,— safe at last. He had passed brilliantly in engineering; had been saved by his prompt and ready answers the consequences of a "fess" with clean black-board in ordnance and gunnery; had won a ringing, though involuntary, round of applause from the crowded galleries of the riding-hall by daring horsemanship, and he was now within seven days of the prized diploma and his commission. "For heaven's sake, Billy," pleaded big Burton, the first captain, "don't do anything to ruin your chances now! I've just been talking with your mother and Miss Nannie, and I declare I never saw that little sister of yours looking so white and worried."

McKay laughs, yet his laugh is not light-hearted.

He wonders if Burton has the faintest intuition that at this moment he is planning an escapade that means nothing short of dismissal if detected. Down in the bottom of his soul he knows he is a fool to have made the rash and boastful pledge to which he now stands committed. Yet he has never "backed out" before, and now—he would dare a dozen dismissals rather than that she should have a chance to say, "I knew you would not come."

That very afternoon, just after the ride in the hall before the Board of Visitors, Miss Waring had been pathetically lamenting that with another week they were to part, and that she had seen next to nothing of him since her arrival.

"If you only *could* get down to Hawkshurst!" she cried. "I'm sure when my cousin Frank was in the corps he used to 'run it' down to Cozzens's to see Cousin Kate,—and that was what made her Cousin Kate to me," she adds, with sudden dropping of the eyelids that is wondrously effective.

"Easily done!" recklessly answers McKay, whose boyish heart is set to hammer-like beating by the closing sentence. "I didn't know you sat up so late there, or I would have come before. Of course I *have* to be here at 'taps.' No one can escape that."

"Oh,—but really, Mr. McKay, I did not mean it! I would not have you run such a risk for worlds! I meant—some other way." And so she protests, although her eyes dance with excitement and delight. What a feather this in her cap of coquetry! What a triumph over the other girls,—especially that hateful set at Craney's! What a delicious confidence to impart to all the little coterie at Hawkshurst! How they must envy her the romance, the danger, the daring, the devotion of such an adventure—for her sake! Of late years such tales had been rare. Girls worth the winning simply would not permit so rash a project, and their example carried weight. But here at "Hawkshurst" was a lively young brood, chaperoned by a matron as wild as her charges and but little older, and eager one and all for any glory or distinction that could pique the pride or stir the envy of " that Craney set." It was too much for a girl of Sallie Waring's type. Her eyes have a dangerous gleam, her cheeks a witching glow; she clings tighter to his arm as she looks up in his face.

"And yet—wouldn't it be lovely?—To think of seeing you there!—are you sure there'd be no danger?"

"Be on the north piazza about quarter of eleven," is the prompt reply. "I'll wear a dark suit, eye-glass, brown moustache, etc. Call me Mr. Freeman while strangers are around. There goes the parade drum. *Au revoir!*" and he darts away. Cadet Captain Stanley, inspecting his company a few moments later, stops in front and gravely rebukes him,—

"You are not properly shaved, McKay."

"I shaved this morning," is the somewhat sullen reply, while an angry flush shoots up towards the blue eyes.

"No razor has touched your upper lip, however, and I expect the class to observe regulations in this company, demerit or no demerit," is the firm, quiet answer, and the young captain passes on to the next man. McKay grits his teeth.

"Only a week more of it, thank God!" he mutters, when sure that Stanley is beyond ear-shot.

Three hours more and "taps" is sounded. All along the brilliant *façade* of barracks there is sudden and simultaneous "dousing of the glim" and a rush of the cadets to their narrow nests. There is a minute of banging doors and hurrying footsteps, and gruff queries of "All in?" as the cadet officers flit from room to room in each division to see that lights are out and every man in bed. Then forth they come from every hall-way; tripping lightly down the stone steps and converging on the guard-house, where stand at the door-way the dark forms of the officer in charge and the cadet officer of the day. Each in turn halts, salutes, and makes his precise report; and when the last sub-division is reported, the executive officer is assured that the battalion of cadets is present in barracks, and at the moment of inspection at least, in bed. Presumably they remain so.

Two minutes after inspection, however, Mr. McKay is out of bed again and fumbling about in his alcove. His room-mate sleepily inquires from beyond the partition what he wants in the dark, but is too long accustomed to his vagaries to expect definite information. When Mr. McKay slips softly out into the hall, after careful *reconnaissance* of the guard-house windows, his chum is soundly asleep and dreaming of no worse freak on Billy's part than a raid around barracks.

It is so near graduation that the rules are relaxed, and in every first classman's room the tailor's handiwork is hanging among the gray uniforms. It is a dark suit of this civilian dress that Billy dons as he emerges from the blankets. A natty Derby is perched upon his curly pate, and a *monocle* hangs by its string. But he cannot light his gas and arrange the soft brown moustache with which he proposes to decorate his upper lip. He must run into Stanley's,—the "tower" room, at the north end of his hall.

Phil looks up from the copy of "Military Law" which he is diligently studying. As "inspector of subdivision," his light is burned until eleven.

"You *do* make an uncommonly swell young cit, Billy," he says, pleasantly. "Doesn't he, Mack?" he continues, appealing to his room-mate, who, lying flat on his back with his head towards the light and a pair of muscular legs in white trousers displayed on top of a pile of blankets, is striving to make out the vacancies in a recent Army Register. "Mack" rolls over and lazily expresses his approval.

"I'd do pretty well if I had my moustache out; I meant to get the start of you fellows, but you're so meanly jealous, you blocked the game, Stan."

All the rancor is gone now. He well knows that Stanley was right.

"Sorry to have had to 'row' you about that, Billy," says the captain, gently. "You know I can't let one man go and not a dozen others."

"Oh, hang it all! What's the difference when time's so nearly up?" responds McKay, as he goes over to the little wood-framed mirror that stands on the iron mantel. "Here's a substitute, though! How's this for a moustache?" he asks, as he turns and faces them. Then he starts for the door. Almost in an instant Stanley is up and after him. Just at the head of the iron stairs he hails and halts him.

"Billy! You are not going out of barracks?"

Unwillingly McKay yields to the pressure of the firm hand laid on his shoulder, and turns.

"Suppose I were, Stanley. What danger is there? Lee inspected last night, and even he wouldn't make such a plan to trip me. Who ever heard of a 'tack's' inspecting after taps two successive nights?"

"There's no reason why it should not be done, and several reasons why it should," is the uncompromising reply. "Don't risk your commission now, Billy, in any mad scheme. Come back and take those things off. Come!"

"Blatherskite! Don't hang on to me like a pickpocket, Stan. Let me go," says McKay, half vexed, half laughing. "I've *got* to go, man," he says, more seriously. "I've promised."

A sudden light seems to come to Stanley. Even in the feeble gleam from the gas-jet in the lower hall McKay can see the look of consternation that shoots across his face.

"You don't mean—you're not going down to Hawkshurst, Billy?"

"Why not to Hawkshurst, if anywhere at all?" is the sullen reply.

"Why? Because you are risking your whole future, —your profession, your good name, McKay. You're risking your mother's heart for the sport of a girl who is simply toying with you——"

"Take care, Stanley. Say what you like to me about myself, but not a word about her."

"This is no time for sentiment, McKay. I have known Miss Waring three years; you, perhaps three weeks. I tell you solemnly that if she has tempted you to 'run it' down there to see her it is simply to boast of a new triumph to the silly pack by whom she is surrounded. I tell you she——"

"You tell me nothing! I don't allow any man to speak in that way of a woman who is my friend," says Billy, with much majesty of mien. "Take your hand off, Stanley," he adds, coldly. "I might have had some respect for your counsel if you had had the least—for my feelings." And wrenching his shoulder away, McKay speeds quickly down the stairs, leaving his comrade speechless and sorrowing in the darkness above.

In the lower hall he stops and peers cautiously over towards the guard-house. The lights are burning brilliantly up in the room of the officer in charge, and the red sash of the officer of the day shows through the open door-way beneath. Now is his time, for there is no one looking. One quick leap through the dim stream of light from the lantern at his back and he will be in the dark area, and can pick his noiseless way to the shadows beyond. It is an easy thing to gain the foot-path beyond the old retaining wall back of the guard-house, scud away under the trees along the winding ascent towards Fort Putnam, until he meets the back-road half-way up the heights; then turn southward through the rocky cuts and forest aisles until he reaches the main highway; then follow on through the beautiful groves, through the quiet village, across the bridge that spans the stream above the falls, and then, only a few hundred yards beyond, there lies Hawkshurst and its bevy of excited, whispering, applauding, delighted girls. If he meet officers, all he has to do is put on a bold face and trust to his disguise. He means to have a glorious time and be back, tingling with satisfaction on his exploit, by a little after midnight. In five minutes his quarrel with Stanley is forgotten, and, all alert and eager, he is half-way up the heights and out of sight or hearing of the barracks.

The roads are well-nigh deserted. He meets one or two squads of soldiers coming back from "pass" at the Falls, but no one else. The omnibuses and carriages bearing home those visitors who have spent the evening listening to the band at the Point are all by this time out of the way, and it is early for officers to be returning from evening calls at the lower hotel. The chances are two to one that he will pass the village without obstacle of any kind. Billy's spirits rise with the occasion, and he concludes that a cigarette is the one thing needful to complete his disguise and add to the general nonchalance of his appearance. Having no matches he waits until he reaches the northern outskirts of the Falls, and then steps boldly into the first bar he sees and helps himself.

Coming forth again he throws wide open the swinging screen doors, and a broad belt of light is flashed across the dusty highway just in front of a rapidly-driven carriage coming north. The mettlesome horses swerve and shy. The occupants are suddenly whirled from their reposeful attitudes, though, fortunately, not from their seats. A "top hat" goes spinning out into the roadway, and a fan flies through the midst of the glare. The driver promptly checks his team and backs them just as Billy, all impulsive courtesy, leaps out into the street; picks up the hat with one hand, the fan with the other, and restores them with a bow to their owners. Only in the nick of time does he recollect himself and crush down the jovial impulse to hail by name Colonel Stanley and his daughter Miriam. The sight of a cavalry uniform and Lieutenant Lee's tall figure on the forward seat has, however, its restraining influence, and he turns quickly away—unrecognized.

But alas for Billy! Only two days before had the distribution been made, and every man in the graduating class was already wearing the beautiful token of their brotherhood. The civilian garb, the Derby hat, the *monocle*, the stick, the cigarette, and the false moustache were all very well in their way, but in the beam of light from the windows of that ill-starred saloon there flashed upon his hand a gem that two pairs of quick, though reluctant eyes could not and did not fail to see,—the *class ring* of 187-.

CHAPTER V.

A MIDNIGHT INSPECTION.

THERE was a sense of constraint among the occupants of Colonel Stanley's carriage as they were driven back to the Point. They had been calling on old friends of his among the pretty villas below the Falls; had been chatting joyously until that sudden swerve that pitched the colonel's hat and Miriam's fan into the dust, and the veteran cavalryman could not account for the lull that followed. Miriam had instantly grasped the situation. All her father's stories of cadet days had enabled her to understand at once that here was a cadet —a classmate of Philip's—" running it" in disguise. Mr. Lee, of course, needed no information on the subject. What she hoped was, that he had not seen ; but the cloud on his frank, handsome face still hovered there, and she knew him too well not to see that he understood everything. And now what was his duty ? Something told her that an inspection of barracks would be made immediately upon his return to the Point, and in that way the name of the absentee be discovered. She knew the regulation every cadet was expected to obey and every officer on honor to enforce. She knew that every cadet found absent from his quarters after taps was called upon by the commandant for prompt account of his whereabouts, and if unable to say that he was on cadet limits during the period of his absence, dismissal stared him in the face.

The colonel did most of the talking on the way back to the south gate. Once within the portals he called to the driver to stop at the Mess. " I'm thirsty," said the jovial warrior, " and I want a julep and a fresh cigar. You, too, might have a claret punch, Mimi ; you are drooping a little to-night. What is it, daughter,— tired ?"

" Yes, tired and a little headachy." Then sudden thought occurs to her. " If you don't mind I think I will go right on to the hotel. Then you and Mr. Lee can enjoy your cigars at leisure." She knows well that Romney Lee is just the last man to let her drive on unescorted. She can hold him ten or fifteen minutes, at least, and by that time if the reckless boy down the road has taken warning and scurried back he can reach the barracks before inspection is made.

"Indeed, Miss Miriam, I'm not to be disposed of so summarily," he promptly answers. "I'll see you safely to the hotel. You'll excuse me, colonel?"

"Certainly, certainly, Lee. I suppose I'll see you later," responds the veteran. They leave him at the Mess and resume their way, and Lee takes the vacated seat by her side. There is something he longs to say to her,—something that has been quivering on his lips and throbbing at his heart for many a long day. She is a queenly woman,—this dark-eyed, stately army girl. It is only two years since, her school-days finished, she has returned to her father's roof on the far frontier and resumed the gay garrison life that so charmed her when a child. Then a loving mother had been her guide, but during her long sojourn at school the blow had fallen that so wrenched her father's heart and left her motherless. Since her graduation she alone has been the joy of the old soldier's home, and sunshine and beauty have again gladdened his life. She would be less than woman did she not know that here now was another soldier, brave, courteous, and gentle, who longed to win her from that home to his own,—to call her by the sacred name of wife. See knew how her father trusted and Phil looked up to him. She knew that down in her own heart of hearts there was pleading for him even now, but as yet no word has been spoken. She is not the girl to signal, "speak, and the prize is yours." He has looked in vain for a symptom that bids him hope for more than loyal friendship.

But to-night as they reach the brightly-lighted piazza at Craney's it is she who bids him stay.

"Don't go just yet," she falters.

"I feared you were tired and wished to go to your room," he answers, gently.

"Would you mind asking if there are letters for me?" she says. It is anything to gain time, and he goes at her behest, but—oh, luckless fate!—'tis a false move.

She sees him stride away through the groups on the piazza; sees the commandant meet him with one of his assistants; sees that there is earnest consultation in low tone, and that then the others hasten down the steps and disappear in the darkness. She hears him say, "I'll follow in a moment, sir," and something tells her that what she dreads has come to pass. Presently he returns to her with the information that there are no letters; then raises his cap, and, in the old Southern and cadet fashion, extends his hand.

"You are not going, Mr. Lee?" again she falters.

"I have to, Miss Stanley."

Slowly she puts forth her hand and lays it in his.

"I—I wish you did not have to go. *Tell* me," she says, impulsively, imploringly, "are you going to inspect?"

He bows his head.

"It is already ordered, Miss Miriam," he says; "I must go at once. Good-night."

Dazed and distressed she turns at once, and is confronted by a pallid little maid with wild, blue eyes.

"Oh, Miss Stanley!" is the wail that greets her. "I could not help hearing, and—if it should be Willy!"

"Come with me, Nannie," she whispers, as her arm enfolds her. "Come to my room."

Meantime, there has been a breeze at the barracks. A batch of yearlings, by way of celebrating their release from plebedom, have hit on a time-honored scheme. Just about the same moment that disclosed to the eyes of Lieutenant Lee the class ring gleaming on the finger of that nattily-dressed young civilian, his comrade, the dozing officer in charge, was started to his feet by a thunder-clap, a vivid flash that lighted up the whole area of barracks, and an explosion that rattled the plaster in the guard-house chimneys. One thing the commandant wouldn't stand was disorder after "taps," and, in accordance with strict instructions, Lieutenant Lawrence sent a drummer-boy at once to find the colonel and tell him what had taken place, while he himself stirred up the cadet officer of the day and began an investigation. Half the corps by this time were up and chuckling with glee at their darkened windows; and as these subdued but still audible demonstrations of sympathy and satisfaction did not cease on his arrival, the colonel promptly sent for his entire force of assistants to conduct the inspection already ordered. Already one or two "bull's-eyes" were flitting out from the officers' angle.

But the piece of boyish mischief that brings such keen delight to the youngsters in the battalion strikes terror to the heart of Philip Stanley. He knows all too well that an immediate inspection will be the result, and then, what is to become of McKay? With keen anxiety, he goes to the hall window overlooking the area, and watches the course of events. A peep into McKay's room shows that he is still absent and that his room-mate, if disturbed at all by the "yearling fireworks," has gone to sleep again. "Stanley sees the commandant stride under the gas-lamp in the area; sees the gathering of the "bull's-eyes," and his heart well-nigh fails him. Still he watches until there can be no doubt that the inspection is already begun. Then, half credulous, all delighted, he notes that it is not Mr. Lee, but young Mr. Lawrence, the officer in charge, who is coming straight towards " B" Company, lantern in hand. Not waiting for the coming of the former, the colonel has directed another officer—not a company commander—to inspect for him.

There is but one way to save Billy now.

In less than half a minute Stanley has darted into McKay's room; has slung his chevroned coat under the bed; has slipped beneath the sheet and coverlet, and now, breathlessly, he listens. He hears the inspector moving from room to room on the ground floor; hears him spring up the iron stair; hears him enter his own, —the tower room at the north end of the hall,—and there he stops, surprised, evidently, to find Cadet Captain Stanley absent from his quarters. Then his steps are heard again. He enters the opposite room at the north end. That is all right! and now he's coming here. "Now for it!" says Stanley to himself, as he throws his white-sleeved arm over his head just as he has so often seen Billy do, and turning his face to the wall, burrows deep in the pillow and pulls the sheet well up to his chin. The door softly opens; the "bull's-eye" flashes its gleam first on one bed, then on the other. "All right here," is the inspector's mental verdict as he pops out again suddenly as he entered. Billy McKay, the scapegrace, is safe and Stanley has time to think over the situation.

At the very worst, as he will be able to say he was "visiting in barracks" when found absent, his own punishment will not be serious. But this is not what troubles him. Demerit for the graduating class ceases to count after the 1st of June, and the individual sense of honor and duty is about the only restraint against lapses of discipline. Stanley hates to think that others may now believe him deaf to this obligation. He would far rather have had this happen when demerit and "confinements" in due proportion had been his award, but there is no use repining. It is a sacrifice to save—her brother.

When half an hour later his classmate, the officer of the day, enters the tower room in search of him, Stanley is there and calmly says, "I was visiting in barracks," in answer to his question; and finally, when morning comes, Mr. Billy McKay nearly sleeps through reveille as a consequence of his night-prowling; but his absence, despite the simultaneous inspection of every company in barracks, has not been detected. With one exception every bed has had its apparently soundly sleeping occupant. The young scamps who caused all the trouble have escaped scot-free, and the corps can hardly believe their own ears, and Billy McKay is stunned and perplexed when it is noised abroad that the only man "hived absent" was the captain of Company "B."

It so happens that both times he goes to find Stanley that day he misses him. "The commandant sent for him an hour ago," says Mr. McFarland, his room-mate, "and I'm blessed if I know what keeps him. Something about last night's doings, I'm afraid."

This, in itself, is enough to make him worry, but the next thing he hears is worse. Just at evening call to quarters, Jim Burton comes to his room.

"Have you heard anything about this report of Stanley's last night?" he asks, and McKay, ordinarily so frank, is guarded now in his reply. For half an hour he has been pacing his room alone. McFarland's revelations have set him to thinking. It is evident that the colonel's suspicions are aroused. It is probable that it is known that some cadet was "running it" the night before. From the simple fact that he is not already in arrest he knows that Mr. Lee did not recognize him, yet the secret has leaked out in some way, and an effort is being made to discover the culprit. Already he has begun to wonder if the game was really worth the candle. He saw her, 'tis true, and had half an hour's whispered chat with her, interrupted not infrequently by giggling and impetuous rushes from the other girls. They had sworn melodramatically never to reveal that it was he who came, but Billy begins to have his doubts. "It ends my career if I'm found out," he reflects, "whereas they can't do much to Stan for visiting." And thus communing with himself, he has decided to guard his secret against all comers,—at least for the present. And so he is non-committal in his reply to Burton.

"What about it?" he asks.

"Why, it's simply this, Billy: Little Magee, the fifer, is on orderly duty to-day, and he heard much of the talk, and I got it out of him. Somebody was running it last night, and was seen down by Cozzens's gate. Stanley was the only absentee, hence Stanley would naturally be the man suspected, but he says he wasn't out of the barracks. The conclusion is inevitable that he was filling the other fellow's place, and the colonel is hopping mad. It looks as though there were collusion between them. Now, Billy, all I've got to say is that the man he's shielding ought to step forward and relieve him at once. There comes the sentry and I must go."

Relieve him? Yes; but what means that for me? thinks poor McKay. Dismissal; a heart break for mother. No! It is too much to face; he must think it over. He never goes near Stanley all that night. He fears to meet him, or the morrow. His heart misgives him when he is told that there has been a long conference in the office. He turns white with apprehension when they fall in for parade, and he notes that it is Phillips, their first lieutenant, who draws sword and takes command of the company; but a few moments later his heart gives one wild bound, then seems to sink into the ground beneath his feet, when the adjutant drops the point of his sword, lets it dangle by the gold knot at his wrist, whips a folded paper from his sash, and far over the plain his clear young voice proclaims the stern order:

"Cadet Captain Stanley is hereby placed in arrest and confined to his quarters. Charge—conniving at concealing the absence of a cadet from inspection after 'taps,' eleven—eleven-fifteen P.M., on the 7th instant.

"By order of Lieutenant-Colonel Putnam."

CHAPTER VI.

THE LAST DANCE.

THE blithest day of all the year has come. The graduating ball takes place to-night. The Point is thronged with joyous visitors, and yet over all there hovers a shadow. In the midst of all this gayety and congratulation there hides a core of sorrow. Voices lower and soft eyes turn in sympathy when certain sad faces are seen. There is one subject on which the cadets simply refuse to talk, and there are two of the graduating class who do not appear at the hotel at all. One is Mr. McKay, whose absence is alleged to be because of confinements he has to serve; the other is Philip Stanley, still in close arrest, and the latter has cancelled his engagements for the ball.

There had been a few days in which Miss McKay, forgetting or having obtained absolution for her unguarded remarks on the promenade deck of the steamer, had begun to be seen a great deal with Miss Stanley. She had even blushingly shaken hands with big Lieutenant Lee, whose kind brown eyes were full of fun and playfulness whenever he greeted her. But it was noticed that something, all of a sudden, had occurred to mar the growing intimacy; then that the once blithe little lady was looking white and sorrowful; that she avoided Miss Stanley for two whole days, and that her blue eyes watched wistfully for some one who did not come,—" Mr. Stanley, no doubt," was the diagnosis of the case by " Miss Mischief" and others.

Then, like a thunder-clap, came the order for Phil Stanley's arrest, and then there were other sad faces. Miriam Stanley's dark eyes were not only troubled, but down in their depths was a gleam of suppressed indignation that people knew not how to explain. Colonel Stanley, to whom every one had been drawn from the first, now appeared very stern and grave; the joy had vanished from his face. Mrs. McKay was flitting about the parlors tearfully thankful that " it wasn't her boy." Nannie had grown whiter still, and very " absent" and silent. Mr. Lee did not come at all.

Then there was startling news! An outbreak, long smouldering, had just occurred at the great reservation of the Spirit Wolf; the agent and several of his men had been massacred, their women carried away into a captivity whose horrors beggar all description, and two troops—hardly sixscore men—of Colonel Stanley's regiment were already in pursuit. Leaving his daughter to the care of an old friend at Craney's, and after a brief interview with his boy at barracks, the old soldier who had come eastward with such glad anticipation turned promptly back to the field of duty. He had taken the first train and was already beyond the Missouri. Almost immediately after the colonel's departure Mr. Lee had come to the hotel and was seen to have a brief but earnest talk with Miss Stanley on the north piazza,—a talk from which she had gone direct to her room and did not reappear for hours, while he, who usually had a genial, kindly word for every one, had turned abruptly down the north steps as though to avoid the crowded halls and piazzas, and so returned to the barracks.

But now, this lovely June morning the news from the far West is still·more direful. Hundreds of savages have taken the war-path, and murder is the burden of every tale from around their reservation, but —this is the day of "last parade" and the graduating ball, and people cannot afford time to think of such grewsome matter. All the same, they note that Mr. Lee comes no more to the hotel, and a rumor is in circulation that he has begged to be relieved from duty at the Point and ordered to join his troop now in the field against hostile Indians.

Nannie McKay is looking like a pathetic shadow of her former self as she comes down-stairs to fulfil an engagement with a cadet admirer. She neglects no duty of the kind towards Willy's friends and hers, but she is drooping and listless. Uncle Jack is worried about her; so, too, is mamma, though the latter is so wrapped up in the graduation of her boy that she has little time to think of pallid cheeks and mournful eyes. It is all arranged that they are to sail for Europe the 1st of July, and the sea air, the voyage across, the new sights and associations on the other side, will "bring her round again," says that observant "avuncular" hopefully. He is compelled to be at his office in the city much of the time, but comes up this day as a matter of course, and has a brief chat with his graceless nephew at the guard-house. Billy's utter lack of spirits sets Uncle Jack to thinking. The boy says he can "tell him nothing just now," and Uncle Jack feels well assured that he has a good deal to tell. He goes in search of Lieutenant Lee, for whom he has conceived a great fancy, but the big lieutenant has gone to the city on business. In the crowded hall at the hotel he meets Miriam Stanley, and her face gives him another pound of trouble to carry.

"You are going to the ball, though?" he hears a lady say to her, and Miriam shakes her head.

Ball, indeed!—or last parade, either! She knows she cannot bear to see the class march to the front, and her brother not there. She cannot bear the thought of even looking on at the ball, if Philip is to be debarred from attending. Her thoughts have been very bitter for a few days past. Her father's intense but silent distress and regret; Philip's certain detention after the graduation of his class; his probable court-martial and loss of rank; the knowledge that he had incurred it all to save McKay (and everybody by this time felt that it *must* be Billy McKay, though no one could prove it), all have conspired to make her very unhappy and very unjust to Mr. Lee. Philip has told her that Mr. Lee had no alternative in reporting to the commandant his discovery "down the road," but she had believed herself of sufficient value in that officer's brown eyes to induce him to at least postpone any mention of that piece of accidental knowledge; and though, in her heart of hearts, she knows she respects him the more because she could not prevail against his sense of duty, she is stung to the quick, and, womanlike, has made him feel it.

It must be in sympathy with her sorrows that, late this afternoon, the heavens open and pour their floods upon the plain. Hundreds of people are bemoaning the fact that now there can be no graduating parade. Down in barracks the members of the class are busily packing trunks, trying on civilian garb, and rushing about in much excitement. In more senses than one Phil Stanley's room is a centre of gravity. The commandant at ten o'clock had sent for him and given him final opportunity to state whose place he occupied during the inspection of that now memorable night, and he had respectfully but firmly declined. There was then no alternative but the withdrawal of his diploma and his detention at the Point to await the action of the Secretary of War upon the charges preferred against him. "The Class," of course, knew by this time that McKay was the man whom he had saved, for after one day of torment and indecision that hapless youth had called in half a dozen of his comrades and made a clean breast of it. It was then his deliberate intention to go to the commandant and beg for Stanley's release, and to offer himself as the culprit. But Stanley had thought the problem out and gravely interposed. It could really do no practical good to him and would only result in disaster to McKay. No one could have anticipated the luckless chain of circumstances that had led to his own arrest, but now he must face the consequences. After long consultation the young counsellors had decided on the plan. "There is only one thing for us to do: keep the matter quiet. There is only one thing for Billy to do: keep a stiff upper lip; graduate with the class, then go to Washington with 'Uncle Jack,' and bestir their friends in Congress,"—not just then assembled, but always available. There was never yet a time when a genuine "pull" from Senate and House did not triumph over the principles of military discipline.

A miserable man is Billy! For a week he has moped in barracks, forbidden by Stanley and his advisers to admit anything, yet universally suspected of being the cause of all the trouble. He, too, wishes to cancel his engagements for the graduating ball, and thinks something ought to be done to those young idiots of yearlings who set off the torpedo. "Nothing could have gone wrong but for them," says he; but the wise heads of the class promptly snub him into silence. "You've simply got to do as we say in this matter, Billy. You've done enough mischief already." And so it results that the message he sends by Uncle Jack is: "Tell mother and Nan I'll meet them at the 'hop.' My confinements end at eight o'clock, but there's no use in my going to the hotel and tramping through the mud." The truth is, he cannot bear to meet Miriam Stanley, and 'twould be just his luck.

One year ago no happier, bonnier, brighter face could have been seen at the Point than that of Nannie McKay. To-night, in all the throng of fair women and lovely girls, gathered with their soldier escort in the great mess-hall, there is none so sad. She tries hard to be chatty and smiling, but is too frank and honest a little soul to have much success. The dances that Phil Stanley had engaged months and months ago are accredited now to other names, and blissful young fellows in gray and gold come successively to claim them. But deep down in her heart she remembers the number of each. It was he who was to have been her escort. It was he who made out her card and gave it to her only a day or two before that fatal interview. It was he who was to have had the last waltz—the very last—that he would dance in the old cadet gray; and though new names have been substituted for his in other cases, this waltz she meant to keep. Well knowing that there would be many to beg for it, she has written Willy's name for "Stanley," and duly warned him of the fact. Then, when it comes, she means to escape to the dressing-room, for she is promptly told that her brother is engaged to Miss Waring for that very waltz. Light as are her feet, she never yet has danced with so heavy a heart. The rain still pours, driving everybody within doors. The heat is intense. The hall is crowded, and it frequently happens that partners cannot find her until near the end of their number on that dainty card. But every one has something to say about Phil Stanley and the universal regret at his absence. It is getting to be more than she can bear,—this prolonged striving to respond with proper appreciation and sympathy, yet not say too much,—not betray the secret that is now burning, throbbing in her girlish heart. He does not dream it, but there, hidden beneath the soft lace upon her snowy neck, lies that "knot of ribbon blue" which she so laughingly had given him, at his urging, the last day of her visit the previous year; the knot which he had so loyally treasured and then so sadly returned. A trifling, senseless thing to make such an ado about, but these hearts are young and ardent, and this romance of his has many a counterpart, the memory of which may bring to war-worn, grizzled heads to-day a blush almost of shame, and would surely bring to many an old and sometimes aching heart a sigh. Hoping against hope, poor Nannie has thought it just possible that at the last moment the authorities would relent and he be allowed to attend. If so,—if so, angry and justly angered though he might be, cut to the heart though he expressed himself, has she not here the means to call him back?—to bid him come and know how contrite she is? Hour after hour she glances at the broad archway at the east, yearning to see his dark, handsome face among the new-comers,—all in vain. Time and again she encounters Sallie Waring, brilliant, bewitching, in the most ravishing of toilets, and always with half a dozen men about her. Twice she notices Will among them with a face gloomy and rebellious, and, hardly knowing why, she almost hates her.

At last comes the waltz that was to have been Philip's,—the waltz she has saved for his sake though he cannot claim it. Mr. Pennock, who has danced the previous galop with her, sees the leader raising his baton, bethinks him of his next partner, and leaves her at the open window close to the dressing-room door. There she can have a breath of fresh air, and, hiding behind the broad backs of several bulky officers and civilians, listen undisturbed to the music she longed to enjoy with him. Here, to her surprise, Will suddenly joins her.

"I thought you were engaged to Miss Waring for this," she says.

"I was," he answers, savagely; "but I'm well out of it. I resigned in favor of a big 'cit' who's worth only twenty thousand a year, Nan, and she has been engaged to him all this time and never let me know until to-night."

"*Willy!*" she gasps. "Oh! I'm so glad—sorry, I mean! I never *did* like her."

"*I* did, Nan, more's the pity. I'm not the first she's made a fool of;" and he turns away, hiding the chagrin in his young face. They are practically alone in this sheltered nook. Crowds are around them, but looking the other way. The rain is dripping from the trees without and pattering on the stone flags. McKay leans out into the night, and the sister's loving heart yearns over him in his trouble.

"Willy," she says, laying the little white-gloved hand on his arm, "it's hard to bear, but she isn't worthy *any* man's love. Twice I've heard in the last two days that she makes a boast of it that 'twas to see her that some one risked his commission and so—kept Mr. Stanley from being here to-night. Willy, *do* you know who it was? *Don't* you think he ought to have come forward like a gentleman, days ago, and told the truth? *Will!* What is it? *Don't* look so! Speak to me, Willy,—your little Nan. Was there ever a time, dear, when my whole heart wasn't open to you in love and sympathy?"

And now, just at this minute, the music begins again. Soft, sweet, yet with such a strain of pathos and of sadness running through every chord; it is the loveliest of all the waltzes played in his "First Class Camp,"—the one of all others he most loved to hear. Her heart almost bursts now to think of him in his lonely room, beyond hearing of the melody that is so

dear to him, that is now so passionately dear to her,—
"Love's Sigh." Doubtless, Philip had asked the
leader days ago to play it here and at no other time.
It is more than enough to start the tears long welling in
her eyes. For an instant it turns her from thought of
Willy's own heartache.

"Will!" she whispers, desperately. "This was to
have been Philip Stanley's waltz—and I want you to
take—something to him for me."

He turns back to her again, his hands clinched, his
teeth set, still thinking only of his own bitter humiliation,—of how that girl has fooled and jilted him,—of
how for her sake he had brought all this trouble on
his stanchest friend.

"Phil Stanley!" he exclaims. "By heaven! it
makes me nearly mad to think of it!—and all for her
sake,—all through me. Oh, Nan! Nan! I *must* tell
you! It was for me,—to save me that——"

"*Willy!*" and there is almost horror in her wide blue
eyes. "*Willy!*" she gasps—"oh, *don't*—don't tell me
that! Oh, it isn't *true?* Not you—not you, Willy.
Not my brother! Oh, quick! Tell me."

Startled, alarmed, he seizes her hand.

"Little sister! What—what has happened—what
is——"

But there is no time for more words. The week of
misery; the piteous strain of the long evening; the
sweet, sad, wailing melody,—his favorite waltz; the
sudden, stunning revelation that it was for Willy's sake
that he—her hero—was now to suffer, he whose heart
she had trampled on and crushed! It is all more than
mortal girl can bear. With the beautiful strains moan-

ing, whirling, ringing, surging through her brain, she is borne dizzily away into darkness and oblivion.

* * * * * * * * *

There follows a week in which sadder faces yet are seen about the old hotel. The routine of the Academy goes on undisturbed. The graduating class has taken its farewell of the gray walls and gone upon its way. New faces, new voices are those in the line of officers at parade. The corps has pitched its white tents under the trees beyond the grassy parapet of Fort Clinton, and, with the graduates and furlough-men gone, its ranks look pitifully thinned. The throng of visitors has vanished. The halls and piazzas at Craney's are well-nigh deserted, but among the few who linger there is not one who has not loving inquiry for the young life that for a brief while has fluttered so near the grave. "Brain fever," said the doctors to Uncle Jack, and a new anxiety was lined in his kindly face as he and Will McKay sped on their mission to the Capitol. They had to go, though little Nan lay sore stricken at the Point.

But youth and elasticity triumph. The danger is passed. She lies now, very white and still, listening to the sweet strains of the band trooping down the line this soft June evening. Her mother, worn with watching, is resting on the lounge. It is Miriam Stanley who hovers at the bedside. Presently the bugles peal the retreat; the sunset gun booms across the plain; the ringing voice of the young adjutant comes floating on the southerly breeze, and, as she listens, Nannie follows every detail of the well-known ceremony, wondering how it *could* go on day after day with no Mr.

Pennock to read the orders; with no "big Burton" to thunder his commands to the first company; with no Philip Stanley to march the colors to their place on the line. " Where is *he?*" is the question in the sweet blue eyes that so wistfully seek his sister's face; but she answers not. One by one the first sergeants made their reports; and now—that ringing voice again, reading the orders of the day. How clear it sounds! How hushed and still the listening Point!

" Head-quarters of the Army," she hears. " Washington, June 15, 187–. Special orders, Number —.

"*First.* Upon his own application, First Lieutenant George Romney Lee, —th Cavalry, is hereby relieved from duty at the U. S. Military Academy, and will join his troop now in the field against hostile Indians.

"*Second.* Upon the recommendation of the Superintendent U. S. Military Academy, the charges preferred against Cadet Captain Philip S. Stanley are withdrawn. Cadet Stanley will be considered as graduated with his class on the 12th instant, will be released from arrest, and authorized to avail himself of the leave of absence granted his class."

Nannie starts from her pillow, clasping in her thin white fingers the soft hand that would have restrained her.

" Miriam!" she cries. " Then—will he go?"

The dark, proud face bends down to her; clasping arms encircle the little white form, and Miriam Stanley's very heart wails forth in answer,—

" Oh, Nannie! He is almost there by this time,— both of them. They left to join the regiment three days ago; their orders came by telegraph."

Another week, and Uncle Jack is again with them. The doctors agree that the ocean voyage is now not only advisable, but necessary. They are to move their little patient to the city and board their steamer in a day or two. Will has come to them, full of disgust that he has been assigned to the artillery, and filling his mother's heart with dismay because he is begging for a transfer to the cavalry, to the —th Regiment,— of all others,—now plunged in the whirl of an Indian war. Every day the papers come freighted with rumors of fiercer fighting; but little that is reliable can be heard from "Sabre Stanley" and his column. They are far beyond telegraphic communication, hemmed in by "hostiles" on every side.

Uncle Jack is an early riser. Going down for his paper before breakfast, he is met at the foot of the stairs by a friend who points to the head-lines of the *Herald*, with the simple remark, "Isn't this hard?"

It is brief enough, God knows.

"A courier just in from Colonel Stanley's camp brings the startling news that Lieutenant Philip Stanley, —th Cavalry, with two scouts and a small escort, who left here Sunday, hoping to push through to the Spirit Wolf, were ambushed by the Indians in Black Cañon. Their bodies, scalped and mutilated, were found Wednesday night."

Where, then, was Romney Lee?

CHAPTER VII.

BLACK CAÑON.

THE red sun is going down behind the line of distant buttes, throwing long shadows out across the grassy upland. Every crest and billow of the prairie is bathed in crimson and gold, while the " breaks" and ravines trending southward grow black and forbidding in their contrasted gloom. Far over to the southeast, in dazzling radiance, two lofty peaks, still snow-clad, gleam against the summer sky, and at their feet dark waves of forest-covered foot-hills drink in the last rays of the waning sunshine as though hoarding its treasured warmth against the chill of coming night. Already the evening air, rare and exhilarating at this great altitude, loses the sun-god's touch and strikes upon the cheek keen as the ether of the limitless heavens. A while ago, only in the distant valley winding to the south could foliage be seen. Now, all in those depths is merged in sombre shade, and not a leaf or tree breaks for miles the grand monotony. Close at hand a host of tiny mounds, each tipped with reddish gold, and some few further ornamented by miniature sentry, alert and keen-eyed, tell of a prairie township already laid out and thickly populated; and at this moment every sentry is chipping his pert, querulous challenge until the disturbers of the peace are close upon him, then diving headlong into the bowels of the earth.

A dun cloud of dust rolls skyward along a well-worn cavalry trail, and is whirled into space by the hoofs of sixty panting chargers trotting steadily south. Sixty sunburned, dust-covered troopers ride grimly on, following the lead of a tall soldier whose kind brown eyes peer anxiously from under his scouting-hat. It is just as they pass the village of the prairie dogs that he points to the low valley down to the front and questions the "plainsman" who lopes along by his side,—

"That Black Cañon down yonder?"

"That's it, lieutenant: I didn't think you could make it to-night."

"We *had* to," is the simple reply as again the spur touches the jaded flank and evokes only a groan in response.

"How far from here to—the Springs?" he presently asks again.

"Box Elder?—where they found the bodies?—'bout five mile, sir."

"Where away was that signal smoke we saw at the divide?"

"Must have been from those bluffs—east of the Springs, sir."

Lieutenant Lee whips out his watch and peers at the dial through the twilight. The cloud deepens on his haggard, handsome face. Eight o'clock, and they have been in saddle almost incessantly since yesterday afternoon, weighed down with the tidings of the fell disaster that has robbed them of their comrades, and straining every nerve to reach the scene.

Only five days before, as he stepped from the railway car at the supply station, a wagon-train had come in from the front escorted by Mr. Lee's own troop; his captain with it, wounded. Just as soon as it could reload with rations and ammunition the train was to start on its eight days' journey to the Spirit Wolf, where Colonel Stanley and the —th were bivouacked and scouring the neighboring mountains. Already a battalion of infantry was at the station, another was on its way, and supplies were being hurried forward. Captain Gregg brought the first reliable news. The Indians had apparently withdrawn from the road. The wagon-train had come through unmolested, and Colonel Stanley was expecting to push forward into their fastnesses farther south the moment he could obtain authority from head-quarters. With these necessary orders two couriers had started just twelve hours before. The captain was rejoiced to see his favorite lieutenant and to welcome Philip Stanley to the regiment. "Everybody seemed to feel that you too would be coming right along," he said; "but, Phil, my boy, I'm afraid you're too late for the fun. You cannot catch the command before it starts from Spirit Wolf."

And yet this was just what Phil had tried to do. Lee knew nothing of his plan until everything had been arranged between the young officer and the major commanding the temporary camp at the station. Then it was too late to protest. While it was Mr. Lee's duty to remain and escort the train, Philip Stanley, with two scouts and half a dozen troopers, had pushed out to overtake the regiment two hundred miles away. Forty-eight hours later, as the wagon-train with its guard was slowly crawling southward, it was met by a courier with ghastly face. He was one of three who had started from the ruined agency together. They met no Indians, but at Box Elder Springs had come upon the bodies of a little party of soldiers stripped, scalped, gashed, and mutilated,—nine in all. There could be little doubt that they were those of poor Philip and his new-found comrades. The courier had recognized two of the bodies as those of Forbes and Whiting,—the scouts who had gone with the party; the others he did not know at all.

Parking his train then and there, sending back to the railway for an infantry company to hasten forward and take charge of it, Mr. Lee never hesitated as to his own course. He and his troop pushed on at once. And now, worn, weary, but determined, the little command is just in sight of the deep ravine known to frontiersmen for years as Black Cañon. It was through here that Stanley and his battalion had marched a fortnight since. It was along this very trail that Phil and his party, pressing eagerly on to join the regiment, rode down into its dark depths and were ambushed at the Springs. From all indications, said the courier, they must have unsaddled for a brief rest, probably just at nightfall; but the Indians had left little to aid them in forming an opinion. Utterly unnerved by the sight, his two associates had turned back to rejoin Stanley's column, while he, the third, had decided to make for the railway. Unless those men, too, had been cut off, the regiment by this time knew of the tragic fate of some of their comrades, but the colonel was mercifully spared all dread that one of the victims was his only son.

Nine were in the party when they started. Nine

bodies were lying there when the couriers reached the Springs, and now nine are lying here to-night when, just after moonrise, Romney Lee dismounts and bends sadly over them, one after another. The prairie wolves have been here first, adding mutilation to the butchery of their human prototypes. There is little chance, in this pallid light and with these poor remnants, to make identification a possibility. All vestiges of uniform, arms, and equipment have been carried away, and such underclothing as remains has been torn to shreds by the herd of snarling, snapping brutes which is driven off only by the rush of the foremost troopers, and is now dispersed all over the cañon and far up the heights beyond the outposts, yelping indignant protest.

There can be no doubt as to the number slain. All the nine are here, and Mr. Lee solemnly pencils the despatch that is to go back to the railway so soon as a messenger and his horse can get a few hours' needed rest. Before daybreak the man is away, meeting on his lonely ride other comrades hurrying to the front, to whom he briefly gives confirmation of the first report. Before the setting of the second sun he has reached his journey's end, and the telegraph is flashing the mournful details to the distant East, and so, when the "Servia" slowly glides from her moorings and turns her prow towards the sparkling sea, Nannie McKay is sobbing her heart out alone in her little white stateroom, crushing with her kisses, bathing with her tears, the love-knot she had given her soldier boy less than a year before.

Another night comes around. Tiny fires are glowing down in the dark depths of Black Cañon, showing red through the frosty gleam of the moonlight. Under the silvery rays nine new-made graves are ranked along the turf, guarded by troopers whose steeds are browsing close at hand. Silence and sadness reign in the little bivouac where Lee and his comrades await the coming of the train they had left three days before. It will be here on the morrow, early, and then they must push ahead and bear their heavy tidings to the regiment. He has written one sorrowing letter—and what a letter to have to write to the woman he loves!—to tell Miriam that he has been unable to identify any one of the bodies as that of her gallant young brother, yet is compelled to believe him to lie there, one of the stricken nine. And now he must face the father with this bitter news! Romney Lee's sore heart fails him at the prospect, and he cannot sleep. Good heaven! *Can* it be that three weeks only have passed away since the night of that lovely yet ill-fated carriage-ride down through Highland Falls, down beyond picturesque Hawkshurst?

Out on the bluffs, though he cannot see them, and up and down the cañon, vigilant sentries guard this solemn bivouac. No sign of Indian has been seen except the hoof-prints of a score of ponies and the bloody relics of their direful visit. No repetition of the signal-smokes has greeted their watchful eyes. It looks as though this outlying band of warriors had noted his coming, had sent up their warning to others of their tribe, and then scattered for the mountains at the south. All the same, as he rode the bluff lines at nightfall, Mr. Lee had charged the sentries to be alert with eye and ear, and to allow none to approach unchallenged.

The weary night wears on. The young moon has ridden down in the west and sunk behind that distant bluff line. All is silent as the graves around which his men are slumbering, and at last, worn with sorrow and vigil, Lee rolls himself in his blanket and, still booted and spurred, stretches his feet towards the little watch-fire, and pillows his head upon the saddle. Down the stream the horses are already beginning to tug at their lariats and struggle to their feet, that they may crop the dew-moistened bunch grass. Far out upon the chill night air the yelping challenge of the coyotes is heard, but the sentries give no sign. Despite grief and care, Nature asserts her sway and is fast lulling Lee to sleep, when, away up on the heights to the northwest, there leaps out a sudden lurid flash and, a second after, the loud ring of the cavalry carbine comes echoing down the cañon. Lee springs to his feet and seizes his rifle. The first shot is quickly followed by a second; the men are tumbling up from their blankets and, with the instinct of old campaigners, thrusting cartridges into the opened chambers.

"Keep your men together here, sergeant," is the brief order, and in a moment more Lee is spurring upward along an old game trail. Just under the crest he overtakes a sergeant hurrying northward.

"What is it? Who fired?" he asks.

"Morris fired, sir: I don't know why. He is the farthest post up the bluffs."

Together they reach a young trooper, crouching in the pallid dawn behind a jagged parapet of rock, and eagerly demanded the cause of the alarm. The sentry is quivering with excitement.

"An Indian, sir! Not a hundred yards out there! I seen him plain enough to swear to it. He rose up from behind that point yonder and started out over the prairie, and I up and fired."

"Did you challenge?"

"No, sir," answers the young soldier, simply. "He was going away. He couldn't understand me if I had, —leastwise I couldn't 'a understood him. He ran like a deer the moment I fired, and was out of sight almost before I could send another shot.

Lee and the sergeant push out along the crest, their arms at "ready," their keen eyes searching every dip in the surface. Close to the edge of the cañon, perhaps a hundred yards away, they come upon a little ledge, behind which, under the bluff, it is possible for an Indian to steal unnoticed towards their sentries and to peer into the depths below. Some one has been here within a few minutes, watching, stretched prone upon the turf, for Lee finds it dry and almost warm, while all around the bunch grass is heavy with dew. Little by little as the light grows warmer in the east and aids them in their search, they can almost trace the outline of a recumbent human form. Presently the west wind begins to blow with greater strength, and they note the mass of clouds, gray and frowning, that is banked against the sky. Out on the prairie not a moving object can be seen, though the eye can reach a good rifle-shot away. Down in the darkness of the cañon the watch-fires still smoulder and the men still wait. There comes no further order from the heights. Lee, with the sergeant, is now bending over faint footprints just discernible in the pallid light.

Suddenly up he starts and gazes eagerly out to the west. The sergeant, too, at the same instant, leaps towards his commander. Distant, but distinct, two quick shots have been fired far over among those tumbling buttes and ridges lying there against the horizon. Before either man could speak or question, there comes another, then another, then two or three in quick succession, the sound of firing thick and fast.

"It's a fight, sir, sure!" cries the sergeant, eagerly.

"To horse, then,—quick!" is the answer, as the two soldiers bound back to the trail.

"Saddle up, men!" rings the order, shouted down the rocky flanks of the ravine. There is instant response in the neigh of excited horses, the clatter of iron-shod hoofs. Through the dim light the men go rushing, saddles and bridles in hand, each to where he has driven his own picket pin. Promptly the steeds are girthed and bitted. Promptly the men come running back to the bivouac, seizing and slinging carbines, then leading into line. A brief word of command, another of caution, and then the whole troop is mounted and, following its leader, rides ghost-like up a winding ravine that enters the cañon from the west and goes spurring to the high plateau beyond. Once there the eager horses have ample room; the springing turf invites their speed. "Front into line" they sweep at rapid gallop, and then, with Lee well out before them, with carbines advanced, with hearts beating high, with keen eyes flashing, and every ear strained for sound of the fray, away they bound. There's a fight ahead! Some one needs their aid, and there's not a man in all old "B" troop who does not mean to avenge those new-made graves. Up a little slope they ride, all eyes fixed on Lee. They see him reach the ridge, sweep gallantly over, then, with ringing cheer, turn in saddle, wave his revolver high in air, clap spur to his horse's flank and go darting down the other side.

"Come *on*, lads!"

Ay, on it is! One wild race for the crest, one headland charge down the slope beyond, and they are rolling over a band of yelling, scurrying, savage horsemen, whirling them away over the opposite ridge, driving them helter-skelter over the westward prairie, until all who escape the shock of the onset or the swift bullet in the raging chase finally vanish from their sight; and then, obedient to the ringing "recall" of the trumpet, slowly they return, gathering again in the little ravine; and there, wondering, rejoicing, jubilant, they cluster at the entrance of a deep cleft in the rocks, where, bleeding from a bullet-wound in the arm, but with a world of thankfulness and joy in his handsome face, their leader stands, clasping Philip Stanley, pallid, faint, well-nigh starved, but—God be praised!—safe and unscathed.

CHAPTER VIII.

CAPTURED.

How the tidings of that timely rescue thrill through every heart at old Fort Warrener! There are gathered the wives and children of the regiment. There is the colonel's home, silent and darkened for that one long week, then ringing with joy and congratulation, with gladness and thanksgiving. Miriam again is there, suddenly lifted from the depths of sorrow to a wealth of bliss she had no words to express. Day and night the little army coterie flocked about her to hear again and again the story of Philip's peril and his final rescue, and then to exclaim over Romney Lee's gallantry and devotion. It was all so bewildering. For a week they had mourned their colonel's only son as dead and buried. The wondrous tale of his discovery sounded simply fabulous, and yet was simply true. Hurrying forward from the railway, the little party had been joined by two young frontiersmen eager to obtain employment with the scouts of Stanley's column. Halting just at sunset for brief rest at Box Elder Springs, the lieutenant with Sergeant Harris had climbed the bluffs to search for Indian signal fires. It was nearly dark when on their return they were amazed to hear the sound of fire-arms in the cañon, and were themselves suddenly attacked and completely cut off from their comrades. Stanley's horse was shot; but Sergeant Harris, though himself wounded, helped his young officer to mount behind him, and galloped back into the darkness, where they evaded their pursuers by turning loose their horse and groping in among the rocks. Here they hid all night and all next day in the deep cleft where Lee had found them, listening to the shouts and signals of a swarm of savage foes. At last the sounds seemed to die away, the Indians to disappear, and then hunger, thirst, and the feverish delirium of the sergeant, who was tortured for want of water, drove Stanley forth in hopes of reaching the cañon. Fired at, as he supposed, by Indians, he was speedily back in his lair again, but was there almost as speedily tracked and besieged. For a while he was able to keep the foe at bay, but Lee had come just in the nick of time; only two cartridges were left, and poor Harris was nearly gone.

A few weeks later, while the —th is still on duty rounding up the Indians in the mountains, the wounded are brought home to Warrener. There are not many, for only the first detachment of two small troops had had any serious engagement; but the surgeons say that Mr. Lee's arm is so badly crippled that he can do no field work for several months, and he had best go in to the railway. And now he is at Warrener; and here, one lovely moonlit summer's evening, he is leaning on the gate in front of the colonel's quarters, utterly regardless of certain injunctions as to avoiding exposure to the night air. Good Mrs. Wilton, the major's wife,—who, army fashion, is helping Miriam keep house in her father's absence,—has gone in before "to light up," she says, though it is too late for callers; and they have been spending a long evening at Captain Gregg's, "down the row." It is Miriam who keeps the tall lieutenant at the gate. She has said good-night, yet lingers. He has been there several days, his arm still in its sling, and not once has she had a word with him alone till now. Some one has told her that he has asked for leave of absence to go East and settle some business affairs he had to leave abruptly when hurrying to take part in the campaign. If this be true is it not time to be making her peace?

The moonlight throws a brilliant sheen on all surrounding objects, yet she stands in the shade, bowered in a little archway of vines that overhangs the gate. He has been strangely silent during the brief walk homeward, and now, so far from following into the shadows as she half hoped he might do, he stands without, the flood of moonlight falling full upon his stalwart figure. Two months ago he would not thus have held aloof, yet now he is half extending his hand as though in adieu. She cannot fathom this strange silence on the part of him who so long has been devoted as a lover. She knows well it cannot be because of her injustice to him at the Point that he is unrelenting now. Her eyes have told him how earnestly she repents: and does he not always read her eyes? Only in faltering words, in the presence of others all too interested, has she been able to speak her thanks for Philip's rescue. She cannot see now that what he fears from her change of mood is that gratitude for her brother's safety, not a woman's response to the passionate love in his deep heart, is the impulse of this sweet, half-shy, half-entreating manner. He cannot sue for love from a girl weighted with a sense of obligation. He knows that lingering here is dangerous, yet he cannot go. When friends are silent 'tis time for chats to close: but there is a silence that at such a time as this only bids a man to speak, and speak boldly. Yet Lee is dumb.

Once—over a year ago—he had come to the colonel's quarters to seek permission to visit the neighboring town on some sudden errand. She had met him at the door with the tidings that her father had been feeling far from well during the morning, and was now taking a nap.

"Won't I do for commanding officer this time?" she had laughingly inquired.

"I would ask no better fate—for all time," was his prompt reply, and he spoke too soon. Though neither ever forgot the circumstance, she would never again permit allusion to it. But to-night it is uppermost in her mind. She *must* know if it be true that he is going.

"Tell me," she suddenly asks, "have you applied for leave of absence?"

"Yes," he answers, simply.

"And you are going—soon?"

"I am going to-morrow," is the utterly unlooked-for reply.

"To-morrow! Why—Mr. Lee!"

There can be no mistaking the shock it gives her, and still he stands and makes no sign. It is cruel of him! What has she said or done to deserve penance like this? He is still holding out his hand as though in adieu, and she lays hers, fluttering, in the broad palm.

"I—I thought all applications had to be made to—your commanding officer," she says at last, falteringly, yet archly.

"Major Wilton forwarded mine on Monday. I asked him to say nothing about it. The answer came by wire to-day."

"Major Wilton is *post* commander; but—did you not—a year——?"

"Did I not?" he speaks in eager joy. "Do you

mean you have not forgotten *that?* Do you mean that now—for all time—my first allegiance shall be to you, Miriam?"

No answer for a minute; but her hand is still firmly clasped in his. At last,—

"Don't you think you ought to have asked me, before applying for leave to go?"

Mr. Lee is suddenly swallowed up in the gloom of that shaded bower under the trellis-work, though a radiance as of mid-day is shining through his heart.

But soon he has to go. Mrs. Wilton is on the veranda, urging them to come in out of the chill night air. Those papers on his desk must be completed and filed this very night. He told her this.

"To-morrow, early, I will be here," he murmurs. "And now, good-night, my own."

But she does not seek to draw her hand away. Slowly he moves back into the bright moonbeams and she follows part way. One quick glance she gives as her hand is released and he raises his forage cap. It is *such* a disadvantage to have but one arm at such a time! She sees that Mrs. Wilton is at the other end of the veranda.

"Good-night," she whispers. "I—know you *must* go."

"I must. There is so much to be done."

"I—thought"—another quick glance at the piazza —"that a soldier, on leaving, should—salute his commanding officer?"

And Romney Lee is again in shadow and—in sunshine.

* * * * * * * * *

Late that autumn, in one of his infrequent letters to his devoted mother, Mr. McKay finds time to allude to the news of Lieutenant Lee's approaching marriage to Miss Stanley.

"Phil is, of course, immensely pleased," he writes, "and from all I hear I suppose Mr. Lee is a very different fellow from what we thought six months ago. Pennock says I always had a wrong idea of him; but Pennock thinks all my ideas about the officers appointed over me are absurd. He likes old Pelican, our battery commander, who is just the crankiest, crabbedest, sore-headedest captain in all the artillery, and that is saying a good deal. I wish I'd got into the cavalry at the start; but there's no use in trying now. The —th is the only regiment I wanted; but they have to go to reveille and stables before breakfast, which wouldn't suit me at all.

"Hope Nan's better. A winter in the Riviera will set her up again. Stanley asks after her when he writes, but he has rather dropped me of late. I suppose it's because I was too busy to answer, though he ought to know that in New York harbor a fellow has no time for scribbling, whereas, out on the plains they have nothing else to do. He sent me his picture a while ago, and I tell you he has improved wonderfully. Such a swell moustache! I meant to have sent it over for you and Nan to see, but I've mislaid it somewhere."

Poor little Nan! She would give many of her treasures for one peep at the coveted picture that Will holds so lightly. There had been temporary improvement in her health at the time Uncle Jack came with the joyous tidings that Stanley was safe after all; but even the Riviera fails to restore her wonted spirits. She droops visibly during the long winter. "She grows so much older away from Willy," says the fond mamma, to whom proximity to that vivacious youth is the acme of earthly bliss. Uncle Jack grins and says nothing. It is dawning upon him that something is needed besides the air and sunshine of the Riviera to bring back the dancing light in those sweet blue eyes and joy to the wistful little face.

"The time to see the Yosemite and 'the glorious climate of California' is April, not October," he suddenly declares, one balmy morning by the Mediterranean; "and the sooner we get back to Yankeedom the better 'twill suit me."

And so it happens that, early in the month of meteorological smiles and tears, the trio are speeding westward far across the rolling prairies: Mrs. McKay deeply scandalized at the heartless conduct of the War Department in refusing Willy a two-months' leave to go with them; Uncle Jack quizzically disposed to look upon that calamity as a not utterly irretrievable ill; and Nan, fluttering with hope, fear, joy, and dread, all intermingled; for is not *he* stationed at Cheyenne? All these long months has she cherished that little knot of senseless ribbon. If she had sent it to him within the week of his graduation, perhaps it would not have seemed amiss; but after that, after all he had been through in the campaign,—the long months of silence, —he might have changed, and, for very shame, she cannot bring herself to give a signal he would perhaps no longer wish to obey. Every hour her excitement and nervousness increase; but when the conductor of the

Pullman comes to say that Cheyenne is really in sight, and the long whistle tells that they are nearing the dinner station of those days, Nan simply loses herself entirely. There will be half an hour, and Philip actually there to see, to hear, to answer. She hardly knows whether she is of this mortal earth when Uncle Jack comes bustling in with the gray-haired colonel, when she feels Miriam's kiss upon her cheek, when Mr. Lee, handsomer and kindlier than ever, bends down to take her hand; but she looks beyond them all for the face she longs for,—and it is not there. The car-seems whirling around when, from over her shoulder, she hears, in the old, well-remembered tones, a voice that redoubles the throb of her little heart.

"Miss Nannie!"

And there—bending over her, his face aglow, and looking marvellously well in his cavalry uniform—is Philip Stanley. She knows not what she says. She has prepared something proper and conventional, but it has all fled. She looks one instant up into his shining eyes, and there is no need to speak at all. Every one else is so busy that no one sees, no one knows, that he is firmly clinging to her hand, and that she shamelessly and passively submits.

A little later—just as the train is about to start— they are standing at the rear door of the sleeper. The band of the —th is playing some distance up the platform,—a thoughtful device of Mr. Lee's to draw the crowd that way,—and they are actually alone. An exquisite happiness is in her eyes as she peers up into the love-light in his strong, steadfast face. *Something* must have been said; for he draws her close to his side and bends over her as though all the world were wrapped up in this dainty little morsel of womanhood. Suddenly the great train begins slowly to move. Part they must now, though it be only for a time. He folds her quickly, unresisting, to his breast. The sweet blue eyes begin to fill.

"My darling,—my little Nannie," he whispers, as his lips kiss away the gathering tears. "There is just an instant. What is it you tell me you have kept for me?"

"This," she answers, shyly placing in his hand a little packet wrapped in tissue-paper. "Don't look at it yet! Wait!—But—I wanted to send it—the very next day, Philip."

Slowly he turns her blushing face until he can look into her eyes. The glory in his proud, joyous gaze is a delight to see. "My own little girl," he whispers, as his lips meet hers. "I know it is my love-knot."

THE WORST MAN IN THE TROOP.

JUST why that young Irishman should have been so balefully branded was more than the first lieutenant of the troop could understand. To be sure, the lieutenant's opportunities for observation had been limited. He had spent some years on detached service in the East, and had joined his comrades in Arizona but a fortnight ago, and here he was already becoming rapidly initiated in the science of scouting through mountain-wilds against the wariest and most treacherous of foemen,— the Apaches of our Southwestern territory.

Coming, as he had done, direct from a station and duties where full-dress uniform, lavish expenditure for kid gloves, bouquets, and Lubin's extracts were matters of daily fact, it must be admitted that the sensations he experienced on seeing his detachment equipped for the scout were those of mild consternation. That much latitude as to individual dress and equipment was permitted he had previously been informed; that "full dress," and white shirts, collars, and the like would be left at home, he had sense enough to know; but that every officer and man in the command would be allowed to discard any and all portions of the regulation uniform and appear rigged out in just such motley guise as his poetic or practical fancy might suggest, had never been pointed out to him; and that he, commanding his troop while a captain commanded the little battalion, could by any military possibility take his place in front of his men without his sabre, had never for an instant occurred to him. As a consequence, when he bolted into the mess-room shortly after daybreak on a bright June morning with that imposing but at most times useless item of cavalry equipment clanking at his heels, the lieutenant gazed with some astonishment upon the attire of his brother-officers there assembled, but found himself the butt of much good-natured and not over-witty "chaff," directed partially at the extreme newness and neatness of his dark-blue flannel scouting-shirt and high-top boots, but more especially at the glittering sabre swinging from his waist-belt.

"Billings," said Captain Buxton, with much solemnity, "while you have probably learned through the columns of a horror-stricken Eastern press that we scalp, alive or dead, all unfortunates who fall into our clutches, I assure you that even for that purpose the cavalry sabre has, in Arizona at least, outlived its usefulness. It is too long and clumsy, you see. What you really want for the purpose is something like this," —and he whipped out of its sheath a rusty but keen-bladed Mexican *cuchillo*,—" something you can wield with a deft turn of the wrist, you know. The sabre is apt to tear and mutilate the flesh, especially when you use both hands." And Captain Buxton winked at the other subaltern and felt that he had said a good thing.

But Mr. Billings was a man of considerable good nature and ready adaptability to the society or circumstances by which he might be surrounded. "Chaff" was a very cheap order of wit, and the serenity of his disposition enabled him to shake off its effect as readily as water is scattered from the plumage of the duck.

"So you don't wear the sabre on a scout? So much the better. I have my revolvers and a Sharp's carbine, but am destitute of anything in the knife line." And with that Mr. Billings betook himself to the duty of despatching the breakfast that was already spread before him in an array tempting enough to a frontier appetite, but little designed to attract a *bon vivant* of civilization. Bacon, *frijoles*, and creamless coffee speedily become ambrosia and nectar under the influence of mountain-air and mountain-exercise; but Mr. Billings had as yet done no climbing. A "buck-board" ride had been his means of transportation to the garrison,—a lonely four-company post in a far-away valley in Northeastern Arizona,—and in the three or four days of intense heat that had succeeded his arrival exercise of any kind had been out of the question. It was with no especial regret, therefore, that he heard the summons of the captain, "Hurry up, man; we must be off in ten minutes." And in less than ten minutes the lieutenant was on his horse and superintending the formation of his troop.

If Mr. Billings was astonished at the garb of his brother-officers at breakfast, he was simply aghast when he glanced along the line of Company "A" (as his command was at that time officially designated) and the first sergeant rode out to report his men present or accounted for. The first sergeant himself was got up in an old gray-flannel shirt, open at and disclosing a broad, brown throat and neck; his head was crowned with what had once been a white felt *sombrero*, now tanned by desert sun, wind, and dirt into a dingy mud-color; his powerful legs were encased in worn deer-skin breeches tucked into low-topped, broad-soled, well-greased boots; his waist was girt with a rude "thimble-belt," in the loops of which were thrust scores of copper cartridges for carbine and pistol; his carbine, and those of all the command, swung in a leather loop athwart the pommel of the saddle; revolvers in all manner of cases hung at the hip, the regulation holster, in most instances, being conspicuous by its absence. Indeed, throughout the entire command the remarkable fact was to be noted that a company of regular cavalry, taking the field against hostile Indians, had discarded pretty much every item of dress or equipment prescribed or furnished by the authorities of the United States, and had supplied themselves with an outfit utterly ununiform, unpicturesque, undeniably slouchy, but not less undeniably appropriate and serviceable. Not a forage-cap was to be seen, not a "campaign-hat" of the style then prescribed by a board of officers that might have known something of hats, but never could have had an idea on the subject of campaigns. Fancy that black enormity of weighty felt, with flapping brim well-nigh a foot in width, absorbing the fiery heat of an Arizona sun, and concentrating the burning rays upon the cranium of its unhappy wearer! No such head-gear would our troopers suffer in the days when General Crook led them through the cañons and deserts of that inhospitable Territory. Regardless of appearances or style himself, seeking only comfort in his dress, the chief speedily found means to indicate that, in Apache-campaigning at least, it was to be a case of *"inter arma silent leges"* in dead earnest; for, freely translated, the old saw read, "No red-tape when Indian-fighting."

Of much of this Lieutenant Billings was only partially informed, and so, as has been said, he was aghast when he marked the utter absence of uniform and the decidedly variegated appearance of his troop. Deerskin, buckskin, canvas, and flannels, leggings, moccasins, and the like, constituted the bill of dress, and old soft felt hats, originally white, the head-gear. If spurs were worn at all, they were of the Mexican variety, easy to kick off, but sure to stay on when wanted. Only two men wore carbine sling-belts, and Mr. Billings was almost ready to hunt up his captain and inquire if by any possibility the men could be attempting to "put up a joke on him," when the captain himself appeared, looking little if any more like the ideal soldier than his men, and the perfectly satisfied expression on his face as he rode easily around, examining closely the horses of the command, paying especial attention to their feet and the shoes thereof, convinced the lieutenant that all was as it was expected to be, if not as it should be, and he swallowed his surprise and held his peace. Another moment, and Captain Wayne's troop came filing past in column of twos, looking, if anything, rougher than his own.

"You follow right after Wayne," said Captain Buxton; and with no further formality Mr. Billings, in a perfunctory sort of way, wheeled his men to the right by fours, broke into column of twos, and closed up on the leading troop.

Buxton was in high glee on this particular morning in June. He had done very little Indian scouting, had been but moderately successful in what he had undertaken, and now, as luck would have it, the necessity arose for sending something more formidable than a mere detachment down into the Tonto Basin, in search of a powerful band of Apaches who had broken loose from the reservation and were taking refuge in the foot-hills of the Black Mesa or among the wilds of the Sierra Ancha. As senior captain of the two, Buxton became commander of the entire force,—two well-filled troops of regular cavalry, some thirty Indian allies as scouts, and a goodly-sized train of pack-mules, with its full complement of packers, *cargadors*, and blacksmiths. He fully anticipated a lively fight, possibly a series of them, and a triumphant return to his post, where hereafter he would be looked up to and quoted as an expert and authority on Apache-fighting. He knew just where the hostiles lay, and was going straight to the point to flatten them out forthwith; and so the little command moved off under admirable auspices and in the best of spirits.

It was a four-days' hard march to the locality where Captain Buxton counted on finding his victims; and when on the fourth day, rather tired and not particularly enthusiastic, the command bivouacked along the banks of a mountain-torrent, a safe distance from the supposed location of the Indian stronghold, he sent forward his Apache Mojave allies to make a stealthy reconnoissance, feeling confident that soon after nightfall they would return with the intelligence that the enemy were lazily resting in their "rancheria," all unsuspicious of his approach, and that at daybreak he would pounce upon and annihilate them.

Soon after nightfall the scouts did return, but their intelligence was not so gratifying: a small—a *very* small —band of renegades had been encamped in that vicinity some weeks before, but not a "hostile" or sign of a hostile was to be found. Captain Buxton hardly slept that night, from disappointment and mortification, and when he went the following day to investigate for himself he found that he had been on a false scent from the start, and this made him crabbed. A week's hunt through the mountains resulted in no better luck, and now, having had only fifteen days' rations at the outset, he was most reluctantly and savagely marching homeward to report his failure.

But Mr. Billings had enjoyed the entire trip. Sleeping in the open air without other shelter than their blankets afforded, scouting by day in single file over miles of mere game-trails, up hill and down dale through the wildest and most dolefully-picturesque scenery he "at least" had ever beheld, under frowning cliffs and beetling crags, through dense forests of pine and juniper, through mountain-torrents swollen with the melting snows of the crests so far above them, through cañons, deep, dark, and gloomy, searching ever for traces of the foe they were ordered to find and fight forthwith, Mr. Billings and his men, having no responsibility upon their shoulders, were happy and healthy as possible, and consequently in small sympathy with their irate leader.

Every afternoon when they halted beside some one of the hundreds of mountain-brooks that came tumbling down from the gorges of the Black Mesa, the men were required to look carefully at the horses' backs and feet, for mountain Arizona is terrible on shoes, equine or human. This had to be done before the herds were turned out to graze with their guard around them; and often some of the men would get a wisp of straw or a suitable wipe of some kind, and thoroughly rub down their steeds. Strolling about among them, as he always did at this time, our lieutenant had noticed a slim but trimly-built young Irishman whose care of and devotion to his horse it did him good to see. No matter how long the march, how severe the fatigue, that horse was always looked after, his grazing-ground pre-empted by a deftly-thrown picket-pin and lariat which secured to him all the real estate that could be surveyed within the circle of which the pin was the centre and the lariat the radius-vector.

Between horse and master the closest comradeship seemed to exist; the trooper had a way of softly singing or talking to his friend as he rubbed him down, and Mr. Billings was struck with the expression and taste with which the little soldier—for he was only five feet five—would render "Molly Bawn" and "Kitty Tyrrell." Except when thus singing or exchanging confidences with his steed, he was strangely silent and reserved; he ate his rations among the other men, yet rarely spoke with them, and he would ride all day through country marvellous for wild beauty and be the only man in the command who did not allow himself to give vent to some expression of astonishment or delight.

"What is that man's name?" asked Mr. Billings of the first sergeant one evening.

"O'Grady, sir," replied the sergeant, with his soldierly salute; and a little later, as Captain Buxton was fretfully complaining to his subaltern of the ill fortune that seemed to overshadow his best efforts, the latter, thinking to cheer him and to divert his attention from his trouble, referred to the troop:

"Why, captain, I don't think I ever saw a finer set of men than you have—anywhere. Now, *there's* a little fellow who strikes me as being a perfect light-cavalry soldier." And the lieutenant indicated his young Irishman.

"You don't mean O'Grady?" asked the captain in surprise.

"Yes, sir,—the very one."

"Why, he's the worst man in the troop."

For a moment Mr. Billings knew not what to say. His captain had spoken with absolute harshness and dislike in his tone of the one soldier of all others who seemed to be the most quiet, attentive, and alert of the troop. He had noticed, too, that the sergeants and the men generally, in speaking to O'Grady, were wont to fall into a kindlier tone than usual, and, though they sometimes squabbled among themselves over the choice of patches of grass for their horses, O'Grady's claim was never questioned, much less "jumped." Respect for his superior's rank would not permit the lieutenant to argue the matter; but, desiring to know more about the case, he spoke again:

"I am very sorry to hear it. His care of his horse and his quiet ways impressed me so favorably."

"Oh, yes, d—n him!" broke in Captain Buxton. "Horses and whiskey are the only things on earth he cares for. As to quiet ways, there isn't a worse devil at large than O'Grady with a few drinks in him. When I came back from two years' recruiting detail he was a sergeant in the troop. I never knew him before, but I soon found he was addicted to drink, and after a while had to ' break' him ; and one night when he was raising hell in the quarters, and I ordered him into the dark cell, he turned on me like a tiger. By Jove! if it hadn't been for some of the men he would have killed me,—or I him. He was tried by court-martial, but most of the detail was made up of infantrymen and staff-officers from Crook's head-quarters, and, by——! they didn't seem to think it any sin for a soldier to threaten to cut his captain's heart out, and Crook himself gave me a sort of a rap in his remarks on the case, and—well, they just let O'Grady off scot-free between them, gave him some little fine, and did more harm than good. He's just as surly and insolent now when I speak to him as he was that night when drunk. Here, I'll show you." And with that Captain Buxton started off towards the herd, Mr. Billings obediently following, but feeling vaguely ill at ease. He had never met Captain Buxton before, but letters from his comrades had prepared him for experiences not altogether pleasant. A good soldier in some respects, Captain Buxton bore the reputation of having an almost ungovernable temper, of being at times brutally violent in his language and conduct towards his men, and, worse yet, of bearing ill-concealed malice, and " nursing his wrath to keep it warm" against such of his enlisted men as had ever ventured to appeal for justice. The captain stopped on reaching the outskirts of the quietly-grazing herd.

"Corporal," said he to the non-commissioned officer

in charge, "isn't that O'Grady's horse off there to the left?"

"Yes, sir."

"Go and tell O'Grady to come here."

The corporal saluted and went off on his errand.

"Now, Mr. Billings," said the captain, "I have repeatedly given orders that my horses must be side-lined when we are in the hostiles' country. Just come here to the left." And he walked over towards a handsome, sturdy little California horse of a bright bay color. "Here, you see, is O'Grady's horse, and not a side-line: that's his way of obeying orders. More than that, he is never content to have his horse in among the others, but must always get away outside, just where he is most apt to be run off by any Indian sharp and quick enough to dare it. Now, here comes O'Grady. Watch him, if you want to see him in his true light."

Standing beside his superior, Mr. Billings looked towards the approaching trooper, who, with a quick, springy step, advanced to within a few yards of them, then stopped short and, erect and in silence, raised his hand in salute, and with perfectly respectful demeanor looked straight at his captain.

In a voice at once harsh and distinctly audible over the entire bivouac, with frowning brow and angry eyes, Buxton demanded,—

"O'Grady, where are your side-lines?"

"Over with my blankets, sir."

"Over with your blankets, are they? Why in——, sir, are they not here on your horse, where they ought to be?" And the captain's voice waxed harsher and louder, and his manner more threatening.

"I understood the captain's orders to be that they need not go on till sunset," replied the soldier, calmly and respectfully, "and I don't like to put them on that sore place, sir, until the last moment."

"Don't like to? No sir, I know d—d well you don't like to obey this or any other order I ever gave, and wherever you find a loop-hole through which to crawl, and you think you can sneak off unpunished, by ——, sir, I suppose you will go on disobeying orders. Shut up, sir! not a d—d word!" for tears of mortification were starting to O'Grady's eyes, and with flushing face and trembling lip the soldier stood helplessly before his troop-commander, and was striving to say a word in further explanation.

"Go and get your side-lines at once and bring them here; go at once, sir," shouted the captain; and with a lump in his throat the trooper saluted, faced about, and walked away.

"He's milder-mannered than usual, d—n him!" said the captain, turning towards his subaltern, who had stood a silent and pained witness of the scene. "He knows he is in the wrong and has no excuse; but he'll break out yet. Come! step out, you O'Grady!" he yelled after the rapidly-walking soldier. "Double time, sir. I can't wait here all night." And Mr. Billings noted that silence had fallen on the bivouac so full of soldier-chaff and laughter but a moment before, and that the men of both troops were intently watching the scene already so painful to him.

Obediently O'Grady took up the "dog-trot" required of him, got his side-lines, and, running back, knelt beside his horse, and with trembling hands adjusted them, during which performance Captain Buxton stood over him, and, in a tone that grew more and more that of a bully as he lashed himself up into a rage, continued his lecture to the man.

The latter finally rose, and, with huge beads of perspiration starting out on his forehead, faced his captain.

"May I say a word, sir?" he asked.

"You may now; but be d—d careful how you say it," was the reply, with a sneer that would have stung an abject slave into a longing for revenge, and that grated on Mr. Billings's nerves in a way that made him clinch his fists and involuntarily grit his teeth. Could it be that O'Grady detected it? One quick, wistful, half-appealing glance flashed from the Irishman's eyes towards the subaltern, and then, with evident effort at composure, but with a voice that trembled with the pent-up sense of wrong and injustice, O'Grady spoke:

"Indeed, sir, I had no thought of neglecting orders. I always care for my horse; but it wasn't sunset when the captain came out——"

"Not sunset!" broke in Buxton, with an outburst of profanity. "Not sunset! why, it's well-nigh dark now, sir, and every man in the troop had side-lined his horse half an hour ago. D—n your insolence, sir! your excuse is worse than your conduct. Mr. Billings, see to it, sir, that this man walks and leads his horse in rear of the troop all the way back to the post. I'll see, by ——! whether he can be taught to obey orders." And with that the captain turned and strode away.

The lieutenant stood for an instant stunned,—simply stunned. Involuntarily he made a step towards O'Grady; their eyes met; but the restraint of discipline was upon both. In that brief meeting of their glances, however, the trooper read a message that was unmistakable.

"Lieutenant ——," he said, but stopped abruptly, pointed aloft over the trees to the eastward with his right hand, dashed it across his eyes, and then, with hurried salute and a choking sort of gurgle in his throat, he turned and went back to his comrades.

Mr. Billings gazed after the retreating form until it disappeared among the trees by the brook-side; then he turned to see what was the meaning of the soldier's pointing over towards the *mesa* to the east.

Down in the deep valley in which the little command had halted for the night the pall of darkness had indeed begun to settle; the bivouac-fires in the timber threw a lurid glare upon the groups gathering around them for supper, and towards the west the rugged upheavals of the Mazatzal range stood like a black barrier against the glorious hues of a bank of summer cloud. All in the valley spoke of twilight and darkness: the birds were still, the voices of the men subdued. So far as local indications were concerned, it *was*—as Captain Buxton had insisted—almost dark. But square over the gilded tree-tops to the east, stretching for miles and miles to their right and left, blazed a vertical wall of rock crested with scrub-oak and pine, every boulder, every tree, glittering in the radiant light of the invisibly setting sun. O'Grady had *not* disobeyed his orders.

Noting this, Mr. Billings proceeded to take a leisurely stroll through the peaceful herd, carefully inspecting each horse as he passed. As a result of his scrutiny, he found that, while most of the horses were already encumbered with their annoying hobble, in "A" Troop alone there were at least a dozen still unfettered, notably the mounts of the non-commissioned officers and the older soldiers. Like O'Grady, they did not wish to inflict the side-line upon their steeds until the last moment. Unlike O'Grady, they had not been called to account for it.

When Mr. Billings was summoned to supper, and he rejoined his brother-officers, it was remarked that he was more taciturn than usual. After that repast had been appreciatively disposed of, and the little group with lighted pipes prepared to spend an hour in chat and contentment, it was observed that Mr. Billings did not take part in the general talk, but that he soon rose, and, out of ear-shot of the officers' camp-fire, paced restlessly up and down, with his head bent forward, evidently plunged in thought.

By and by the half-dozen broke up and sought their blankets. Captain Buxton, somewhat mollified by a good supper, was about rolling into his "Navajo," when Mr. Billings stepped up:

"Captain, may I ask for information as to the side-line order? After you left this evening, I found that there must be some misunderstanding about it."

"How so?" said Buxton, shortly.

"In this, captain;" and Mr. Billings spoke very calmly and distinctly. "The first sergeant, several other non-commissioned officers and men,—more than a dozen, I should say,—did not side-line their horses until half an hour after you spoke to O'Grady, and the first sergeant assured me, when I called him to account for it, that your orders were that it should be done at sunset."

"Well, by ——! it was after sunset—at least it was getting mighty dark—when I sent for that blackguard O'Grady," said Buxton, impetuously, "and there is no excuse for the rest of them."

"It was beginning to grow dark down in this deep valley, I know, sir; but the tree-tops were in a broad glare of sunlight while we were at the herd, and those cliffs for half an hour longer."

"Well, Mr. Billings, I don't propose to have any hair-splitting in the management of my troop," said the captain, manifestly nettled. "It was practically sunset to us when the light began to grow dim, and my men know it well enough." And with that he rolled over and turned his back to his subaltern.

Disregarding the broad hint to leave, Mr. Billings again spoke:

"Is it your wish, sir, that any punishment should be imposed on the men who were equally in fault with O'Grady?"

Buxton muttered something unintelligible from under his blankets.

"I did not understand you, sir," said the lieutenant, very civilly.

Buxton savagely propped himself up on one elbow, and blurted out,—

"No, Mr. Billings! no! When I want a man punished I'll give the order myself, sir."

"And is it still your wish, sir, that I make O'Grady walk the rest of the way?"

For a moment Buxton hesitated; his better nature

struggled to assert itself and induce him to undo the injustice of his order; but the "cad" in his disposition, the weakness of his character, prevailed. It would never do to let his lieutenant get the upper hand of him, he argued, and so the reply came, and came angrily.

"Yes, of course; he deserves it anyhow, by ——! and it'll do him good."

Without another word Mr. Billings turned on his heel and left him.

The command returned to garrison, shaved its stubbly beard of two weeks' growth, and resumed its uniform and the routine duties of the post. Three days only had it been back when Mr. Billings, marching on as officer of the day, and receiving the prisoners from his predecessor, was startled to hear the list of names wound up with "O'Grady," and when that name was called there was no response.

The old officer of the day looked up inquiringly: "Where is O'Grady, sergeant?"

"In the cell, sir, unable to come out.

"O'Grady was confined by Captain Buxton's order late last night," said Captain Wayne, "and I fancy the poor fellow has been drinking heavily this time."

A few minutes after, the reliefs being told off, the prisoners sent out to work, and the officers of the day, new and old, having made their reports to the commanding officer, Mr. Billings returned to the guardhouse, and, directing his sergeant to accompany him, proceeded to make a deliberate inspection of the premises. The guard-room itself was neat, clean, and dry; the garrison prison-room was well ventilated, and tidy as such rooms ever can be made; the Indian prison-room, despite the fact that it was empty and every shutter was thrown wide open to the breeze, had that indefinable, suffocating odor which continued aboriginal occupancy will give to any apartment; but it was the cells Mr. Billings desired to see, and the sergeant led him to a row of heavily-barred doors of rough unplaned timber, with a little grating in each, and from one of these gratings there peered forth a pair of feverishly-glittering eyes, and a face, not bloated and flushed, as with recent and heavy potations, but white, haggard, twitching, and a husky voice in piteous appeal addressed the sergeant:

"Oh, for God's sake, Billy, get me something, or it'll kill me!"

"Hush, O'Grady," said the sergeant: "here's the officer of the day."

Mr. Billings took one look at the wan face only dimly visible in that prison-light, for the poor little man shrank back as he recognized the form of his lieutenant:

"Open that door, sergeant."

With alacrity the order was obeyed, and the heavy door swung back upon its hinges.

"O'Grady," said the officer of the day, in a tone gentle as that he would have employed in speaking to a woman, "come out here to me. I'm afraid you are sick."

Shaking, trembling, twitching in every limb, with wild, dilated eyes and almost palsied step, O'Grady came out.

"Look to him a moment, sergeant," said Mr. Billings, and, bending low, he stepped into the cell. The atmosphere was stifling, and in another instant he backed out into the hall-way. "Sergeant, was it by the commanding officer's order that O'Grady was put in there?"

"No, sir; Captain Buxton's."

"See that he is not returned there during my tour, unless the orders come from Major Stannard. Bring O'Grady into the prison-room."

Here in the purer air and brighter light he looked carefully over the poor fellow, as the latter stood before him quivering from head to foot and hiding his face in his shaking hands. Then the lieutenant took him gently by the arm and led him to a bunk:

"O'Grady, man, lie down here. I'm going to get something that will help you. Tell me one thing: how long had you been drinking before you were confined?"

"About forty-eight hours, sir, off and on."

"How long since you ate anything?"

"I don't know, sir; not for two days, I think."

"Well, try and lie still. I'm coming back to you in a very few minutes."

And with that Mr. Billings strode from the room, leaving O'Grady, dazed, wonder-stricken, gazing stupidly after him.

The lieutenant went straight to his quarters, took a goodly-sized goblet from the painted pine sideboard, and with practised hand proceeded to mix therein a beverage in which granulated sugar, Angostura bitters, and a few drops of lime-juice entered as minor ingredients, and the coldest of spring-water and a brimming measure of whiskey as constituents of greater quality and quantity. Filling with this mixture a small leather-covered flask, and stowing it away within the breast-pocket of his blouse, he returned to the guard-house, musing as he went, "'If this be treason,' said Patrick Henry, 'make the most of it.' If this be conduct prejudicial, etc., say I, do your d—dest. That man would be in the horrors of jim-jams in half an hour more if it were not for this." And so saying to himself, he entered the prison-room, called to the sergeant to bring him some cold water, and then approached O'Grady, who rose unsteadily and strove to stand attention, but the effort was too much, and again he covered his face with his arms, and threw himself in utter misery at the foot of the bunk.

Mr. Billings drew the flask from his pocket, and, touching O'Grady's shoulder, caused him to raise his head:

"Drink this, my lad. I would not give it to you at another time, but you need it now."

Eagerly it was seized, eagerly drained, and then, after he had swallowed a long draught of the water, O'Grady slowly rose to his feet, looking, with eyes rapidly softening and losing their wild glare, upon the young officer who stood before him. Once or twice he passed his hands across his forehead, as though to sweep away the cobwebs that pressed upon his brain, but for a moment he did not essay a word. Little by little the color crept back to his cheek; and, noting this, Mr. Billings smiled very quietly, and said, "Now, O'Grady, lie down; you will be able to sleep now until the men come in at noon; then you shall have another drink, and you'll be able to eat what I send you. If you cannot sleep, call the sergeant of the guard; or if you want anything, I'll come to you."

Then, with tears starting to his eyes, the soldier found words: "I thank the lieutenant. If I live a thousand years, sir, this will never be forgotten,—never, sir! I'd have gone crazy without your help, sir."

Mr. Billings held out his hand, and, taking that of his prisoner, gave it a cordial grip: "That's all right, O'Grady. Try to sleep now, and we'll pull you through. Good-by, for the present." And, with a heart lighter, somehow, than it had been of late, the lieutenant left.

At noon that day, when the prisoners came in from labor and the officer's of the day inspected their general condition before permitting them to go to their dinner, the sergeant of the guard informed him that O'Grady had slept quietly almost all the morning, but was then awake and feeling very much better, though still weak and nervous.

"Do you think he can walk over to my quarters?" asked Mr. Billings.

"He will try it, sir, or anything the lieutenant wants him to try."

"Then send him over in about ten minutes."

Home once more, Mr. Billings started a tiny blaze in his oil-stove, and soon had a kettle of water boiling merrily. Sharp to time a member of the guard tapped at the door, and, on being bidden "Come in," entered, ushering in O'Grady; but meantime, by the aid of a little pot of meat-juice and some cayenne pepper, a glass of hot soup or beef-tea had been prepared, and, with some dainty slices of potted chicken and the accompaniments of a cup of fragrant tea and some ship-biscuit, was in readiness on a little table in the back room.

Telling the sentinel to remain in the shade on the piazza, the lieutenant proceeded first to make O'Grady sit down in a big wicker arm-chair, for the man in his broken condition was well-nigh exhausted by his walk across the glaring parade in the heat of an Arizona noonday sun. Then he mixed and administered the counterpart of the beverage he had given his prisoner-patient in the morning, only in point of potency it was an evident falling off, but sufficient for the purpose, and in a few minutes O'Grady was able to swallow his breakfast with evident relish, meekly and unhesitatingly obeying every suggestion of his superior.

His breakfast finished, O'Grady was then conducted into a cool, darkened apartment, a back room in the lieutenant's quarters.

"Now, pull off your boots and outer clothing, man, spread yourself on that bed, and go to sleep, if you can. If you can't, and you want to read, there are books and papers on that shelf; pin up the blanket on the window, and you'll have light enough. You shall not be disturbed, and I know you won't attempt to leave."

"Indeed, sir, I won't," began O'Grady, eagerly; but the lieutenant had vanished, closing the door after him, and a minute later the soldier had thrown himself upon the cool, white bed, and was crying like a tired child.

Three or four weeks after this incident, to the small regret of his troop and the politely-veiled indifference of the commissioned element of the garrison, Captain Buxton concluded to avail himself of a long-deferred "leave," and turned over his company property to Mr.

Billings in a condition that rendered it necessary for him to do a thing that "ground" him, so to speak: he had to ask several favors of his lieutenant, between whom and himself there had been no cordiality since the episode of the bivouac, and an open rupture since Mr. Billings's somewhat eventful tour as officer of the day, which has just been described.

It appeared that O'Grady had been absent from no duty (there were no drills in that scorching June weather), but that, yielding to the advice of his comrades, who knew that he had eaten nothing for two days and was drinking steadily into a condition that would speedily bring punishment upon him, he had asked permission to be sent to the hospital, where, while he could get no liquor, there would be no danger attendant upon his sudden stop of all stimulant. The first sergeant carried his request with the sick-book to Captain Buxton, O'Grady meantime managing to take two or three more pulls at the bottle, and Buxton, instead of sending him to the hospital, sent for him, inspected him, and did what he had no earthly authority to do, directed the sergeant of the guard to confine him at once in the dark cell.

"It will be no punishment as he is now," said Buxton to himself, "but it will be hell when he wakes."

And so it had been; and far worse it probably would have been but for Mr. Billings's merciful interference.

Expecting to find his victim in a condition bordering upon the abject and ready to beg for mercy at any sacrifice of pluck or pride, Buxton had gone to the guard-house soon after retreat and told the sergeant that he desired to see O'Grady, if the man was fit to come out.

What was his surprise when the soldier stepped forth in his trimmest undress uniform, erect and steady, and stood unflinchingly before him!—a day's rest and quiet, a warm bath, wholesome and palatable food, careful nursing, and the kind treatment he had received having brought him round with a sudden turn that he himself could hardly understand.

"How is this?" thundered Buxton. "I ordered you kept in the dark cell."

"The officer of the day ordered him released, sir," said the sergeant of the guard.

And Buxton, choking with rage, stormed into the mess-room, where the younger officers were at dinner, and, regardless of the time, place, or surroundings, opened at once upon his subaltern:

"Mr. Billings, by whose authority did you release O'Grady from the dark cell?"

Mr. Billings calmly applied his napkin to his moustache, and then as calmly replied, "By my own, Captain Buxton."

"By ——! sir, you exceeded your authority."

"Not at all, captain; on the contrary, you exceeded yours."

At this Buxton flew into a rage that seemed to deprive him of all control over his language. Oaths and imprecations poured from his lips; he raved at Billings, despite the efforts of the officers to quiet him, despite the adjutant's threat to report his language at once to the commanding officer.

Mr. Billings paid no attention whatever to his accusations, but went on eating his dinner with an appearance of serenity that only added fuel to his captain's fire. Two or three officers rose and left the table in disgust, and just how far the thing might have gone cannot be accurately told, for in less than three minutes there came a quick, bounding step on the piazza, the clank and rattle of a sabre, and the adjutant fairly sprang back into the room:

"Captain Buxton, you will go at once to your quarters in close arrest, by order of Major Stannard."

Buxton knew his colonel and that little fire-eater of an adjutant too well to hesitate an instant. Muttering imprecations on everybody, he went.

The next morning, O'Grady was released and returned to duty. Two days later, after a long and private interview with his commanding officer, Captain Buxton appeared with him at the officers' mess at dinner-time, made a formal and complete apology to Lieutenant Billings for his offensive language, and to the mess generally for his misconduct; and so the affair blew over; and, soon after, Buxton left, and Mr. Billings became commander of Troop "A."

And now, whatever might have been his reputation as to sobriety before, Private O'Grady became a marked man for every soldierly virtue. Week after week he was to be seen every fourth or fifth day, when his guard tour came, reporting to the commanding officer for duty as "orderly," the nattiest, trimmest soldier on the detail.

"I always said," remarked Captain Wayne, "that Buxton alone was responsible for that man's downfall; and this proves it. O'Grady has all the instincts of a

p

gentleman about him, and now that he has a gentleman over him he is himself again."

One night, after retreat-parade, there was cheering and jubilee in the quarters of Troop "A." Corporal Quinn had been discharged by expiration of term of service, and Private O'Grady was decorated with his chevrons. When October came, the company muster-roll showed that he had won back his old grade; and the garrison knew no better soldier, no more intelligent, temperate, trustworthy non-commissioned officer, than Sergeant O'Grady. In some way or other the story of the treatment resorted to by his amateur medical officer had leaked out. Whether faulty in theory or not, it was crowned with the verdict of success in practice; and, with the strong sense of humor which pervades all organizations wherein the Celt is represented as a component part, Mr. Billings had been lovingly dubbed "Doctor" by his men, and there was one of their number who would have gone through fire and water for him.

One night some herdsmen from up the valley galloped wildly into the post. The Apaches had swooped down, run off their cattle, killed one of the cowboys, and scared off the rest. At daybreak the next morning Lieutenant Billings, with Troop "A" and about a dozen Indian scouts, was on the trail, with orders to pursue, recapture the cattle, and punish the marauders.

To his disgust, Mr. Billings found that his allies were not of the tribes who had served with him in previous expeditions. All the trusty Apache Mojaves and Hualpais were off with other commands in distant parts of the Territory. He had to take just what the agent could give him at the reservation,—some Apache Yumas, who were total strangers to him. Within forty-eight hours four had deserted and gone back; the others proved worthless as trailers, doubtless intentionally, and had it not been for the keen eye of Sergeant O'Grady it would have been impossible to keep up the pursuit by night; but keep it up they did, and just at sunset, one sharp autumn evening, away up in the mountains, the advance caught sight of the cattle grazing along the shores of a placid little lake, and, in less time than it takes to write it, Mr. Billings and his command tore down upon the quarry, and, leaving a few men to "round up" the herd, were soon engaged in a lively running fight with the fleeing Apaches which lasted until dark, when the trumpet sounded the recall, and, with horses somewhat blown, but no casualties of importance, the command reassembled and marched back to the grazing-ground by the lake. Here a hearty supper was served out, the horses were rested, then given a good "feed" of barley, and at ten o'clock Mr. Billings with his second lieutenant and some twenty men pushed ahead in the direction taken by the Indians, leaving the rest of the men under experienced non-commissioned officers to drive the cattle back to the valley.

That night the conduct of the Apache Yuma scouts was incomprehensible. Nothing would induce them to go ahead or out on the flanks; they cowered about the rear of column, yet declared that the enemy could not be hereabouts. At two in the morning Mr. Billings found himself well through a pass in the mountains, high peaks rising to his right and left, and a broad valley in front. Here he gave the order to unsaddle and camp for the night.

At daybreak all were again on the alert: the search for the trail was resumed. Again the Indians refused to go out without the troops; but the men themselves found the tracks of Tonto moccasins along the bed of a little stream purling through the cañon, and presently indications that they had made the ascent of the mountain to the south. Leaving a guard with his horses and pack-mules, the lieutenant ordered up his men, and soon the little command was silently picking its way through rock and boulder, scrub-oak and tangled juniper and pine. Rougher and steeper grew the ascent; more and more the Indians cowered, huddling together in rear of the soldiers. Twice Mr. Billings signalled a halt, and, with his sergeants, fairly drove the scouts up to the front and ordered them to hunt for signs. In vain they protested, "No sign,—no Tonto here;" their very looks belied them, and the young commander ordered the search to be continued. In their eagerness the men soon leaped ahead of the wretched allies, and the latter fell back in the same huddled group as before.

After half an hour of this sort of work, the party came suddenly upon a point whence it was possible to see much of the face of the mountain they were scaling. Cautioning his men to keep within the concealment afforded by the thick timber, Mr. Billings and his comrade-lieutenant crept forward and made a brief reconnoissance. It was evident at a glance that the farther they went the steeper grew the ascent and the more tangled the low shrubbery, for it was little better, until, near the summit, trees and underbrush, and herbage of every description, seemed to cease entirely, and a vertical cliff of jagged rocks stook sentinel at the crest, and stretched east and west the entire length of the face of the mountain.

"By Jove, Billings! if they are on top of that it will be a nasty place to rout them out of," observed the junior.

"I'm going to find out where they are, anyhow," replied the other. "Now those infernal Yumas have *got* to scout, whether they want to or not. You stay here with the men, ready to come the instant I send or signal."

In vain the junior officer protested against being left behind; he was directed to send a small party to see if there were an easier way up the hill-side farther to the west, but to keep the main body there in readiness to move whichever way they might be required. Then, with Sergeant O'Grady and the reluctant Indians, Mr. Billings pushed up to the left front, and was soon out of sight of his command. For fifteen minutes he drove his scouts, dispersed in skirmish order, ahead of him, but incessantly they sneaked behind rocks and trees out of his sight; twice he caught them trying to drop back, and at last, losing all patience, he sprang forward, saying, "Then *come* on, you whelps, if you cannot lead," and he and the sergeant hurried ahead. Then the Yumas huddled together again and slowly followed.

Fifteen minutes more, and Mr. Billings found himself standing on the edge of a broad shelf of the mountain,—a shelf covered with huge boulders of rock tumbled there by storm and tempest, riven by lightning-stroke or the slow disintegration of nature from the bare, glaring, precipitous ledge he had marked from below. East and west it seemed to stretch, forbidding and inaccessible. Turning to the sergeant, Mr. Billings directed him to make his way off to the right and see if there were any possibility of finding a path to the summit; then looking back down the side, and marking his Indians cowering under the trees some fifty yards away, he signalled "come up," and was about moving farther to his left to explore the shelf, when something went whizzing past his head, and, embedding itself in a stunted oak behind him, shook and quivered with the shock,—a Tonto arrow. Only an instant did he see it, photographed as by electricity upon the retina, when with a sharp stinging pang and whirring " whist" and thud a second arrow, better aimed, tore through the flesh and muscles just at the outer corner of his left eye, and glanced away down the hill. With one spring he gained the edge of the shelf, and shouted to the scouts to come on. Even as he did so, bang! bang! went the reports of two rifles among the rocks, and, as with one accord, the Apache Yumas turned tail and rushed back down the hill, leaving him alone in the midst of hidden foes. Stung by the arrow, bleeding, but not seriously hurt, he crouched behind a rock, with carbine at ready, eagerly looking for the first sign of an enemy. The whiz of another arrow from the left drew his eyes thither, and quick as a flash his weapon leaped to his shoulder, the rocks rang with its report, and one of the two swarthy forms he saw among the boulders tumbled over out of sight; but even as he threw back his piece to reload, a rattling volley greeted him, the carbine dropped to the ground, a strange, numbed sensation had seized his shoulder, and his right arm, shattered by a rifle-bullet, hung dangling by the flesh, while the blood gushed forth in a torrent.

Defenceless, he sprang back to the edge; there was nothing for it now but to run until he could meet his men. Well he knew they would be tearing up the mountain to the rescue. Could he hold out till then? Behind him with shout and yells came the Apaches, arrow and bullet whistling over his head; before him lay the steep descent,—jagged rocks, thick, tangled bushes: it was a desperate chance; but he tried it, leaping from rock to rock, holding his helpless arm in his left hand; then his foot slipped: he plunged heavily forward; quickly the nerves threw out their signal for support to the muscles of the shattered member, but its work was done, its usefulness destroyed. Missing its support, he plunged heavily forward, and went crashing down among the rocks eight or ten feet below, cutting a jagged gash in his forehead, while the blood rained down into his eyes and blinded him; but he struggled up and on a few yards more; then another fall, and, well-nigh senseless, utterly exhausted, he lay groping for his revolver,—it had fallen from its case. Then—all was over.

Not yet; not yet. His ear catches the sound of a voice he knows well,—a rich, ringing, Hibernian voice it is: "Lieutenant, *lieutenant!* Where are ye?" and he has strength enough to call, "This way, sergeant, this way," and in another moment O'Grady, with blended anguish and gratitude in his face, is bending over him. "Oh, thank God you're not kilt, sir!" (for when excited O'Grady *would* relapse into the brogue); "but are ye much hurt?"

"Badly, sergeant, since I can't fight another round."

"Then put your arm round my neck, sir," and in a second the little Patlander has him on his brawny back. But with only one arm by which to steady himself, the other hanging loose, the torture is inexpressible, for O'Grady is now bounding down the hill, leaping like a goat from rock to rock, while the Apaches with savage yells come tearing after them. Twice, pausing, O'Grady lays his lieutenant down in the shelter of some large boulder, and, facing about, sends shot after shot up the hill, checking the pursuit and driving the cowardly footpads to cover. Once he gives vent to a genuine Kilkenny "hurroo" as a tall Apache drops his rifle and plunges headforemost among the rocks with his hands convulsively clasped to his breast. Then the sergeant once more picks up his wounded comrade, despite pleas, orders, or imprecations, and rushes on.

"I cannot stand it, O'Grady. Go and save yourself. You *must* do it. I *order* you to do it." Every instant the shots and arrows whiz closer, but the sergeant never winces, and at last, panting, breathless, having carried his chief full three hundred yards down the rugged slope, he gives out entirely, but with a gasp of delight points down among the trees:

"Here come the boys, sir."

Another moment, and the soldiers are rushing up the rocks beside them, their carbines ringing like merry music through the frosty air, and the Apaches are scattering in every direction.

"Old man, are you much hurt?" is the whispered inquiry his brother-officer can barely gasp for want of breath, and, reassured by the faint grin on Mr. Billings's face, and a barely audible "Arm busted,—that's all; pitch in and use them up," he pushes on with his men.

In ten minutes the affair is ended. The Indians have been swept away like chaff; the field and the wounded they have abandoned are in the hands of the troopers; the young commander's life is saved; and then, and for long after, the hero of the day is Buxton's *bête noire*, "the worst man in the troop."

VAN.

HE was the evolution of a military horse-trade,—one of those periodical swappings required of his dragoons by Uncle Sam on those rare occasions when a regiment that has been dry-rotting half a decade in Arizona is at last relieved by one from the Plains. How it happened that we of the Fifth should have kept him from the clutches of those sharp horse-fanciers of the Sixth is more than I know. Regimental tradition had it that we got him from the Third Cavalry when it came our turn to go into exile in 1871. He was the victim of some temporary malady at the time,—one of those multitudinous ills to which horse-flesh is heir,—or he never would have come to us. It was simply impossible that anybody who knew anything about horses should trade off such a promising young racer so long as there remained an unpledged pay-account in the officers' mess. Possibly the arid climate of Arizona had disagreed with him and he had gone amiss, as would the mechanism of some of the best watches in the regiment, unable to stand the strain of anything so hot and high and dry. Possibly the Third was so overjoyed at getting out of Arizona on any terms that they would gladly have left their eye-teeth in pawn. Whatever may have been the cause, the transfer was an accomplished fact, and Van was one of some seven hundred quadrupeds, of greater or less value, which became the property of the Fifth Regiment of Cavalry, U.S.A., in lawful exchange for a like number of chargers left in the stables along the recently-built Union Pacific to await the coming of their new riders from the distant West.

We had never met in those days, Van and I. "Compadres" and chums as we were destined to become, we were utterly unknown and indifferent to each other; but in point of regimental reputation at the time, Van had decidedly the best of it. He was a celebrity at head-quarters, I a subaltern at an isolated post. He had apparently become acclimated, and was rapidly winning respect for himself and dollars for his backers; I was winning neither for anybody, and doubtless losing both,—they go together, somehow. Van was living on metaphorical clover down near Tucson; I was roughing it out on the rocks of the Mogollon. Each after his own fashion served out his time in the grim old Territory, and at last "came marching home again;" and early in the summer of the Centennial year, and just in the midst of the great Sioux war of 1876, Van and I made each other's acquaintance.

What I liked about him was the air of thoroughbred ease with which he adapted himself to his surroundings. He was in swell society on the occasion of our first meeting, being bestridden by the colonel of the regiment. He was dressed and caparisoned in the height of martial fashion; his clear eyes, glistening coat, and joyous bearing spoke of the perfection of health; his every glance and movement told of elastic vigor and dauntless spirit. He was a horse with a pedigree,—let alone any self-made reputation,—and he knew it; more than that, he knew that I was charmed at the first greeting; probably he liked it, possibly he liked me. What he saw in me I never discovered. Van, though demonstrative eventually, was reticent and little given to verbal flattery. It was long indeed before any degree of intimacy was established between us: perhaps it might never have come but for the strange and eventful campaign on which we were so speedily launched. Probably we might have continued on our original status of dignified and distant acquaintance. As a member of the colonel's household he could have nothing in common with me or mine, and his acknowledgment of the introduction of my own charger—the cavalryman's better half—was of that airy yet perfunctory politeness which is of the club clubby. Forager, my gray, had sought acquaintance in his impulsive frontier fashion when summoned to the presence of the regimental commander, and, ranging alongside to permit the shake of the hand with which the colonel had honored his rider, he himself had with equine confidence addressed Van, and Van had simply continued his dreamy stare over the springy prairie and taken no earthly notice of him. Forager and I had just joined regimental head-quarters for the first time, as was evident, and we were both "fresh." It was not until the colonel good-naturedly stroked the glossy brown neck of his pet and said, " Van, old boy, this is Forager, of ' K' Troop," that Van considered it the proper thing to admit my fellow to the outer edge of his circle of acquaintance. My gray thought him a supercilious snob, no doubt, and hated him. He hated him more before the day was half over, for the colonel decided to gallop down the valley to look at some new horses that had just come, and invited me to go. Colonels' invitations are commands, and we went, Forager and I, though it was weariness and vexation of spirit to both. Van and his rider flew easily along, bounding over the springy turf with long, elastic stride, horse and rider taking the rapid motion as an everyday matter, in a cool, imperturbable, this-is-the-way-we-always-do-it style; while my poor old troop-horse, in answer to pressing knee and pricking spur, strove with panting breath and jealously bursting heart to keep alongside. The foam flew from his fevered jaws and flecked the smooth flank of his apparently unconscious rival; and when at last we returned to camp, while Van, without a turned hair or an abnormal heave, coolly nodded off to his stable, poor Forager, blown, sweating, and utterly used up, gazed revengefully after him an instant and then reproachfully at me. He had done his best, and all to no purpose. That confounded clean-cut, supercilious beast had worn him out and never tried a spurt.

It was then that I began to make inquiries about that airy fellow Van, and I soon found he had a history. Like other histories, it may have been a mere codification of lies; but the men of the Fifth were ready to answer for its authenticity, and Van fully looked the character they gave him. He was now in his prime. He had passed the age of tell-tale teeth and was going on between eight and nine, said the knowing ones, but he looked younger and felt younger. He was at heart as full of fun and frolic as any colt, but the responsibilities of his position weighed upon him at times and lent to his elastic step the grave dignity that should mark the movements of the first horse of the regiment.

And then Van was a born aristocrat. He was not impressive in point of size; he was rather small, in fact; but there was that in his bearing and demeanor that attracted instant attention. He was beautifully built,—lithe, sinewy, muscular, with powerful shoulders and solid haunches; his legs were what Oscar Wilde might have called poems, and with better reason than when he applied the epithet to those of Henry Irving: they were straight, slender, and destitute of those heterodox developments at the joints that render equine legs as hideous deformities as knee-sprung trousers of the present mode. His feet and pasterns were shapely and dainty as those of the *señoritas* (only for pastern read ankle) who so admired him on *festa* days at Tucson, and who won such stores of *dulces* from the scowling gallants who had with genuine Mexican pluck backed the Sonora horses at the races. His color was a deep, dark chocolate-brown; a most unusual tint, but Van was proud of its oddity, and his long, lean head, his pretty little pointed ears, his bright, flashing eye and sensitive nostril, one and all spoke of spirit and intelligence. A glance at that horse would tell the veriest greenhorn that speed, bottom, and pluck were all to be found right there; and he had not been in the regiment a month before the knowing ones were hanging about the Mexican sports and looking out for a chance for a match; and Mexicans, like Indians, are consummate horse-racers.

Not with the "greasers" alone had tact and diplomacy to be brought into play. Van, though invoiced as a troop-horse sick, had attracted the attention of the colonel from the very start, and the colonel had speedily caused him to be transferred to his own stable, where, carefully tended, fed, groomed, and regularly exercised, he speedily gave evidence of the good there was in him. The colonel rarely rode in those days, and cavalry-duties in garrison were few. The regiment was in the mountains most of the time, hunting Apaches, but Van had to be exercised every day; and exercised he was. "Jeff," the colonel's orderly, would lead him sedately forth from his paddock every morning about nine, and ride demurely off towards the quartermaster's stables in rear of the garrison. Keen eyes used to note that Van had a way of sidling along at such times as though his heels were too impatient to keep at their appropriate distance behind the head, and "Jeff's" hand on the bit was very firm, light as it was.

"Bet you what you like those 'L' Company fellows are getting Van in training for a race," said the quartermaster to the adjutant one bright morning, and the chuckle with which the latter received the remark was an indication that the news was no news to him.

"If old Coach don't find it out too soon, some of these swaggering *caballeros* around here are going to lose their last winnings," was his answer. And, true to their cavalry instincts, neither of the staff-officers saw fit to follow Van and his rider beyond the gate to the *corrals*.

Once there, however, Jeff would bound off quick as

a cat, Van would be speedily taken in charge by a squad of old dragoon sergeants, his cavalry bridle and saddle exchanged for a light racing-rig, and Master Mickey Lanigan, son and heir of the regimental saddle-sergeant, would be hoisted into his throne, and then Van would be led off, all plunging impatience now, to an improvised race-track across the *arroyo*, where he would run against his previous record, and where old horses from the troop-stables would be spurred into occasional spurts with the champion, while all the time vigilant "non-coms" would be thrown out as pickets far and near, to warn off prying Mexican eyes and give notice of the coming of officers. The colonel was always busy in his office at that hour, and interruptions never came. But the race did, and more than one race, too, occurring on Sundays, as Mexican races will, and well-nigh wrecking the hopes of the garrison on one occasion because of the colonel's sudden freak of holding a long mounted inspection on that day. Had he ridden Van for two hours under his heavy weight and housings that morning, all would have been lost. There was terror at Tucson when the cavalry trumpets blew the call for mounted inspection, full dress, that placid Sunday morning, and the sporting sergeants were well-nigh crazed. Not an instant was to be lost. Jeff rushed to the stable, and in five minutes had Van's near fore foot enveloped in a huge poultice, much to Van's amaze and disgust, and when the colonel came down,

> Booted and spurred and prepared for a ride,

there stood Jeff in martial solemnity, holding the colonel's other horse, and looking, as did the horse, the picture of dejection.

"What'd you bring me that infernal old hearse-horse for?" said the colonel. "Where's Van?"

"In the stable, dead lame, general," said Jeff, with face of woe, but with diplomatic use of the brevet. "Can't put his nigh fore foot to the ground, sir. I've got it poulticed, sir, and he'll be all right in a day or two——"

"Sure it ain't a nail?" broke in the colonel, to whom nails in the foot were sources of perennial dread.

"Perfectly sure, general," gasped Jeff. "D—d sure!" he added, in a tone of infinite relief, as the colonel rode out on the broad parade. "'Twould 'a' been nails in the coffins of half the Fifth Cavalry if it *had* been."

But that afternoon, while the colonel was taking his siesta, half the populace of the good old Spanish town of Tucson was making the air blue with *carambas* when Van came galloping under the string an easy winner over half a score of Mexican steeds. The "dark horse" became a notoriety, and for once in its history head-quarters of the Fifth Cavalry felt the forthcoming visit of the paymaster to be an object of indifference.

Van won other races in Arizona. No more betting could be got against him around Tucson; but the colonel went off on leave, and he was borrowed down at Camp Bowie awhile, and then transferred to Crittenden, —only temporarily, of course, for no one at head-quarters would part with him for good. Then, when the regiment made its homeward march across the continent in 1875, Van somehow turned up at the *festa* races at

Albuquerque and Santa Fé, though the latter was off the line of march by many miles. Then he distinguished himself at Pueblo by winning a handicap sweepstakes where the odds were heavy against him. And so it was that when I met Van at Fort Hays in May, 1876, he was a celebrity. Even then they were talking of getting him down to Dodge City to run against some horses on the Arkansaw; but other and graver matters turned up. Van had run his last race.

Early that spring, or rather late in the winter, a powerful expedition had been sent to the north of Fort Fetterman in search of the hostile bands led by that dare-devil Sioux chieftain Crazy Horse. On "Patrick's Day in the morning," with the thermometer indicating 30° below, and in the face of a biting wind from the north and a blazing glare from the sheen of the untrodden snow, the cavalry came in sight of the Indian encampment down in the valley of Powder River. The fight came off then and there, and, all things considered, Crazy Horse got the best of it. He and his people drew away farther north to join other roving bands. The troops fell back to Fetterman to get a fresh start; and when spring fairly opened, old "Gray Fox," as the Indians called General Crook, marched a strong command up to the Big Horn Mountains, determined to have it out with Crazy Horse and settle the question of supremacy before the end of the season. Then all the unoccupied Indians in the North decided to take a hand. All or most of them were bound by treaty obligations to keep the peace with the government that for years past had fed, clothed, and protected them. Nine-tenths of those who rushed to the rescue of Crazy

Horse and his people had not the faintest excuse for their breach of faith; but it requires neither eloquence nor excuse to persuade the average Indian to take the war-path. The reservations were beset by vehement old strifemongers preaching a crusade against the whites, and by early June there must have been five thousand eager young warriors, under such leaders as Crazy Horse, Gall, Little Big Man, and all manner of Wolves, Bears, and Bulls, and prominent among the latter that head-devil, scheming, lying, wire-pulling, big-talker-but-no-fighter, Sitting Bull,—" Tatanka-e-Yotanka,"—five thousand fierce and eager Indians, young and old, swarming through the glorious upland between the Big Horn and the Yellowstone, and more a-coming.

Crook had reached the head-waters of Tongue River with perhaps twelve hundred cavalry and infantry, and found that something must be done to shut off the rush of reinforcements from the southeast. Then it was that we of the Fifth, far away in Kansas, were hurried by rail through Denver to Cheyenne, marched thence to the Black Hills to cut the trails from the great reservations of Red Cloud and Spotted Tail to the disputed ground of the Northwest; and here we had our own little personal tussle with the Cheyennes, and induced them to postpone their further progress towards Sitting Bull and to lead us back to the reservation. It was here, too, we heard how Crazy Horse had pounced on Crook's columns on the bluffs of the Rosebud that sultry morning of the 17th of June and showed the Gray Fox that he and his people were too weak in numbers to cope with them. It was here, too, worse luck, we got the tidings of the dread disaster of the Sunday one week later, and listened in awed silence to the story of Custer's mad attack on ten times his weight in foes—and the natural result. Then came our orders to hasten to the support of Crook, and so it happened that July found us marching for the storied range of the Big Horn, and the first week in August landed us, blistered and burned with sun-glare and stifling alkali-dust, in the welcoming camp of Crook.

Then followed the memorable campaign of 1876. I do not mean to tell its story here. We set out with ten days' rations on a chase that lasted ten weeks. We roamed some eighteen hundred miles over range and prairie, over "bad lands" and worse waters. We wore out some Indians, a good many soldiers, and a great many horses. We sometimes caught the Indians, and sometimes they caught us. It was hot, dry summer weather when we left our wagons, tents, and extra clothing; it was sharp and freezing before we saw them again; and meantime, without a rag of canvas or any covering to our backs except what summer-clothing we had when we started, we had tramped through the valleys of the Rosebud, Tongue, and Powder Rivers, had loosened the teeth of some men with scurvy before we struck the Yellowstone, had weeded out the wounded and ineffective there and sent them to the East by river, had taken a fresh start and gone rapidly on in pursuit of the scattering bands, had forded the Little Missouri near where the Northern Pacific now spans the stream, run out of rations entirely at the head of Heart River, and still stuck to the trail and the chase, headed southward over rolling, treeless prairies, and for eleven days and nights of pelting, pitiless rain dragged our way through the bad-lands, meeting and fighting the Sioux two lively days among the rocks of Slim Buttes, subsisting meantime partly on what game we could pick up, but mainly upon our poor, famished, worn-out, staggering horses. It is hard truth for cavalryman to tell, but the choice lay between them and our boots· and most of us had no boots left by the time we sighted the Black Hills. Once there, we found provisions and plenty; but never, I venture to say, never was civilized army in such a plight as was the command of General George Crook when his brigade of regulars halted on the north bank of the Belle Fourche in September, 1876. Officers and men were ragged, haggard, half starved, worn down to mere skin and bone; and the horses,—ah, well, only half of them were left: hundreds had dropped starved and exhausted on the line of march, and dozens had been killed and eaten. We had set out blithe and merry, riding jauntily down the wild valley of the Tongue. We straggled in towards the Hills, towing our tottering horses behind us: they had long since grown too weak to carry a rider.

Then came a leisurely saunter through the Hills. Crook bought up all the provisions to be had in Deadwood and other little mining towns, turned over the command to General Merritt, and hastened to the forts to organize a new force, leaving to his successor instructions to come in slowly, giving horses and men time to build up. Men began "building up" fast enough; we did nothing but eat, sleep, and hunt grass for our horses for whole weeks at a time; but our horses,—ah, that was different. There was no grain to be had for them. They had been starving for a month, for the Indians had burned the grass before us wherever we went, and here in the pine-covered hills what grass could be found was scant and wiry,—not the rich, juicy, strength-giving bunch grass of the open country. Of my two horses, neither was in condition to do military duty when we got to Whitewood. I was adjutant of the regiment, and had to be bustling around a good deal; and so it happened that one day the colonel said to me, "Well, here's Van. He can't carry my weight any longer. Suppose you take him and see if he won't pick up." And that beautiful October day found the racer of the regiment, though the ghost of his former self, transferred to my keeping.

All through the campaign we had been getting better acquainted, Van and I. The colonel seldom rode him, but had him led along with the head-quarters party in the endeavor to save his strength. A big, raw-boned colt, whom he had named "Chunka Witko," in honor of the Sioux "Crazy Horse," the hero of the summer, had the honor of transporting the colonel over most of those weary miles, and Van spent the long days on the muddy trail in wondering when and where the next race was to come off, and whether at this rate he would be fit for a finish. One day on the Yellowstone I had come suddenly upon a quartermaster who had a peck of oats on his boat. Oats were worth their weight in greenbacks, but so was plug tobacco. He gave me half a peck for all the tobacco in my saddle-bags, and, filling my old campaign hat with the precious grain, I sat me down on a big log by the flowing Yellowstone and told poor old "Donnybrook" to pitch in. "Donnybrook" was a "spare horse" when we started on the campaign, and had been handed over to me after the fight on the War Bonnet, where Merritt turned their own tactics on the Cheyennes. He was sparer still by this time; and later, when we got to the muddy banks of the " Heecha Wapka," there was nothing to spare of him. The head-quarters party had dined on him the previous day, and only groaned when that Mark Tapley of a surgeon remarked that if this was Donnybrook Fare it was tougher than all the stories ever told of it. Poor old Donnybrook! He had recked not of the coming woe that blissful hour by the side of the rippling Yellowstone. His head was deep in my lap, his muzzle buried in oats; he took no thought for the morrow,—he would eat, drink, and be merry, and ask no questions as to what was to happen; and so absorbed were we in our occupation—he in his happiness, I in the contemplation thereof—that neither of us noticed the rapid approach of a third party until a whinny of astonishment sounded close beside us, and Van, trailing his lariat and picket-pin after him, came trotting up, took in the situation at a glance, and, unhesitatingly ranging alongside his comrade of coarser mould and thrusting his velvet muzzle into my lap, looked wistfully into my face with his great soft brown eyes and pleaded for his share. Another minute, and, despite the churlish snappings and threatening heels of Donnybrook, Van was supplied with a portion as big as little Benjamin's, and, stretching myself beside him on the sandy shore, I lay and watched his enjoyment. From that hour he seemed to take me into his confidence, and his was a friendship worth having. Time and again on the march to the Little Missouri and southward to the Hills he indulged me with some slight but unmistakable proof that he held me in esteem and grateful remembrance. It may have been only a bid for more oats, but he kept it up long after he knew there was not an oat in Dakota,—that part of it, at least. But Van was awfully pulled down by the time we reached the pine-barrens up near Deadwood. The scanty supply of forage there obtained (at starvation price) would not begin to give each surviving horse in the three regiments a mouthful. And so by short stages we plodded along through the picturesque beauty of the wild Black Hills, and halted at last in the deep valley of French Creek. Here there was grass for the horses and rest for the men.

For a week now Van had been my undivided property, and was the object of tender solicitude on the part of my German orderly, "Preuss," and myself. The colonel had chosen for his house the foot of a big pine-tree up a little ravine, and I was billeted alongside a fallen ditto a few yards away. Down the ravine, in a little clump of trees, the head-quarters stables were established, and here were gathered at nightfall the chargers of the colonel and his staff. Custer City, an almost deserted village, lay but a few miles off to the west, and thither I had gone the moment I could get leave, and my mission was oats. Three stores were still open, and, now that the troops had come swarming down, were doing a thriving business. Whiskey, tobacco, bottled beer, canned lobster, canned anything, could be had in profusion, but not a grain of oats, barley, or corn. I went over to a miner's wagon-train and offered ten dollars for a sack of oats.

The boss teamster said he would not sell oats for a cent apiece if he had them, and so sent me back down the valley sore at heart, for I knew Van's eyes, those great soft brown eyes, would be pleading the moment I came in sight; and I knew more,—that somewhere the colonel had " made a raise," that he *had* one sack, for Preuss had seen it, and Chunka Witko had had a peck of oats the night before and another that very morning. Sure enough, Van was waiting, and the moment he saw me coming up the ravine he quit his munching at the scanty herbage, and, with ears erect and eager eyes, came quickly towards me, whinnying welcome and inquiry at the same instant. Sugar and hard-tack, delicacies he often fancied in prosperous times, he took from my hand even now; he was too truly a gentleman at heart to refuse them when he saw they were all I had to give; but he could not understand why the big colt should have his oats and he, Van, the racer and the hero of two months ago, should starve, and I could not explain it.

That night Preuss came up and stood attention before my fire, where I sat jotting down some memoranda in a note-book:

" Lieutenant, I kent shtaendt ut no longer yet. Dot scheneral's horse he git oats ag'in diesen abent, unt Ven, he git noddings, unt he look, unt look. He ot dot golt unt den ot me look, unt I *couldn't* shtaendt ut, lieutenant——"

And Preuss stopped short and winked hard and drew his ragged shirt-sleeve across his eyes.

Neither could I " shtaendt ut." I jumped up and went to the colonel and begged a hatful of his precious oats, not for my sake, but for Van's. "Self-preservation is the first law of nature," and your own horse before that of all the world is the cavalryman's creed. It was a heap to ask, but Van's claim prevailed, and down the dark ravine "in the gloaming" Preuss and I hastened with eager steps and two hats full of oats; and that rascal Van heard us laugh, and answered with impatient neigh. He knew we had not come empty-handed this time.

Next morning, when every sprig and leaf was glistening in the brilliant sunshine with its frosty dew, Preuss led Van away up the ravine to picket him on a little patch of grass he had discovered the day before, and as he passed the colonel's fire a keen-eyed old veteran of the cavalry service, who had stopped to have a chat with our chief, dropped the stick on which he was whittling and stared hard at our attenuated racer.

"Whose horse is that, orderly?" he asked.

"De *etschudant's*, colonel," said Preuss, in his labored dialect.

"The adjutant's! Where did he get him? Why, that horse is a runner!" said "Black Bill," appreciatively.

And pretty soon Preuss came back to me, chuckling. He had not smiled for six weeks.

"Ven—he veels pully dis morning," he explained. "Dot Colonel Royle he shpeak mit him unt pet him, unt Ven, he laeff unt gick up mit his hint lecks. He git vell bretty gwick yet."

Two days afterwards we broke up our bivouac on French Creek, for every blade of grass was eaten off, and pushed over the hills to its near neighbor, Amphibious Creek, an eccentric stream whose habit of diving into the bowels of the earth at unexpected turns and disappearing from sight entirely, only to come up surging and boiling some miles farther down the valley, had suggested its singular name. "It was half land, half water," explained the topographer of the first expedition that had located and named the streams in these jealously-guarded haunts of the red men. Over on Amphibious Creek we were joined by a motley gang of recruits just enlisted in the distant cities of the East and sent out to help us fight Indians. One out of ten might know how to load a gun, but as frontier soldiers not one in fifty was worth having. But they brought with them capital horses, strong, fat, grain-fed, and these we campaigners levied on at once. Merritt led the old soldiers and the new horses down into the valley of the Cheyenne on a chase after some scattering Indian bands, while "Black Bill" was left to hammer the recruits into shape and teach them how to care for invalid horses. Two handsome young sorrels had come to me as my share of the plunder, and with these for alternate mounts I rode the Cheyenne raid, leaving Van to the fostering care of the gallant old cavalryman who had been so struck with his points the week previous.

One week more, and the reunited forces of the expedition, Van and all, trotted in to "round up" the semi-belligerent warriors at the Red Cloud agency on White River, and, as the war-ponies and rifles of the scowling braves were distributed among the loyal scouts, and dethroned Machpealota (old Red Cloud) turned over the government of the great Sioux nation, Ogallallas and all, to his more reliable rival, Sintegaliska,—

Spotted Tail,—Van surveyed the ceremony of abdication from between my legs, and had the honor of receiving an especial pat and an admiring "*Washtay*" from the new chieftain and lord of the loyal Sioux. His highness Spotted Tail was pleased to say that he wouldn't mind swapping four of his ponies for Van, and made some further remarks which my limited knowledge of the Brulé Dakota tongue did not enable me to appreciate as they deserved. The fact that the venerable chieftain had hinted that he might be induced to throw in a spare squaw "to boot" was therefore lost, and Van was saved. Early November found us, after an all-summer march of some three thousand miles, once more within sight and sound of civilization. Van and I had taken station at Fort D. A. Russell, and the bustling prairie city of Cheyenne lay only three miles away. Here it was that Van became my pet and pride. Here he lived his life of ease and triumph, and here, gallant fellow, he met his knightly fate.

Once settled at Russell, all the officers of the regiment who were blessed with wives and children were speedily occupied in getting their quarters ready for their reception; and late in November my own little household arrived and were presented to Van. He was then domesticated in a rude but comfortable stable in rear of my little army-house, and there he slept, was groomed and fed, but never confined. He had the run of our yard, and, after critical inspection of the wood-shed, the coal-hole, and the kitchen, Van seemed to decide upon the last-named as his favorite resort. He looked with curious and speculative eyes upon our darky cook on the arrival of that domestic functionary, and seemed for once in his life to be a trifle taken aback by the sight of her woolly pate and Ethiopian complexion. Hannah, however, was duly instructed by her mistress to treat Van on all occasions with great consideration, and this to Hannah's darkened intellect meant unlimited loaf-sugar. The adjutant could not fail to note that Van was almost always to be seen standing at the kitchen door, and on those rare occasions when he himself was permitted to invade those premises he was never surprised to find Van's shapely head peering in at the window, or head, neck, and shoulders bulging in at the wood-shed beyond.

Yet the ex-champion and racer did not live an idle existence. He had his hours of duty, and keenly relished them. Office-work over at orderly-call, at high noon it was the adjutant's custom to return to his quarters and speedily to appear in riding-dress on the front piazza. At about the same moment Van, duly caparisoned, would be led forth from his paddock, and in another moment he and his rider would be flying off across the breezy level of the prairie. Cheyenne, as has been said, lay just three miles away, and thither Van would speed with long, elastic strides, as though glorying in his powers. It was at once his exercise and his enjoyment, and to his rider it was the best hour of the day. He rode alone, for no horse at Russell could keep alongside. He rode at full speed, for in all the twenty-four that hour from twelve to one was the only one he could call his own for recreation and for healthful exercise. He rode to Cheyenne that he might be present at the event of the day,—the arrival of the trans-continental train from the East.

He sometimes rode beyond, that he might meet the train when it was belated and race it back to town; and this—*this* was Van's glory. The rolling prairie lay open and free on each side of the iron track, and Van soon learned to take his post upon a little mound whence the coming of the "express" could be marked, and, as it flared into sight from the darkness of the distant snow-shed, Van, all a-tremble with excitement, would begin to leap and plunge and tug at the bit and beg for the word to go. Another moment, and, carefully held until just as the puffing engine came well alongside, Van would leap like arrow from the string, and away we would speed, skimming along the springy turf. Sometimes the engineer would curb his iron horse and hold him back against the "down-grade" impetus of the heavy Pullmans far in rear; sometimes he would open his throttle and give her full head, and the long train would seem to leap into space, whirling clouds of dust from under the whirling wheels, and then Van would almost tear his heart out to keep alongside.

Month after month through the sharp mountain winter, so long as the snow was not whirling through the air in clouds too dense to penetrate, Van and his master had their joyous gallops. Then came the spring, slow, shy, and reluctant as the springtide sets in on that high plateau in mid-continent, and Van had become even more thoroughly domesticated. He now looked upon himself as one of the family, and he knew the dining-room window, and there, thrice each day and sometimes at odd hours between, he would take his station while the household was at table and plead with those great soft brown eyes for sugar. Commissary-bills ran high that winter, and cut loaf-sugar was an item of untold expenditure. He had found a new ally and friend,—a little girl with eyes as deep and dark as and browner than his own, a winsome little maid of three, whose golden, sunshiny hair floated about her bonny head and sweet serious face like a halo of light from another world. Van "took to her" from the very first. He courted the caress of her little hand, and won her love and trust by the discretion of his movements when she was near. As soon as the days grew warm enough, she was always out on the front piazza when Van and I came home from our daily gallop, and then she would trot out to meet us and be lifted to her perch on the pommel; and then, with mincing gait, like lady's palfrey, stepping as though he might tread on eggs and yet not crush them, Van would take the little one on her own share of the ride. And so it was that the loyal friendship grew and strengthened. The one trick he had was never ventured upon when she was on his back, even after she became accustomed to riding at rapid gait and enjoying the springy canter over the prairie before Van went back to his stable. It was a strange trick: it proved a fatal one.

No other horse I ever rode had one just like it. Running at full speed, his hoofs fairly flashing through the air and never seeming to touch the ground, he would suddenly, as it were, "change step" and gallop "disunited," as we cavalrymen would say. At first I thought it must be that he struck some rolling stone, but soon I found that when bounding over the soft turf it was just the same; and the men who knew him in the days of his prime in Arizona had noted it there. Of course there was nothing to do for it but make him change back as quick as possible on the run, for Van was deaf to remonstrance and proof against the rebuke of spur. Perhaps he could not control the fault; at all events he did not, and the effect was not pleasant. The rider felt a sudden jar, as though the horse had come down stiff-legged from a hurdle-leap; and sometimes it would be so sharp as to shake loose the forage-cap upon his rider's head. He sometimes did it when going at easy lope, but never when his little girl-friend was on his back; then he went on springs of air.

One bright May morning all the different "troops," as the cavalry-companies are termed, were out at drill on the broad prairie. The colonel was away, the officer of the day was out drilling his own company, the adjutant was seated in his office hard at work over regimental papers, when in came the sergeant of the guard, breathless and excited.

"Lieutenant," he cried, "six general prisoners have escaped from the guard-house. They have got away down the creek towards town."

In hurried question and answer the facts were speedily brought out. Six hard customers, awaiting sentence after trial for larceny, burglary, assault with intent to kill, and finally desertion, had been cooped up together in an inner room of the ramshackle old wooden building that served for a prison, had sawed their way through to open air, and, timing their essay by the sound of the trumpets that told them the whole garrison would be out at morning drill, had slipped through the gap at the right moment, slid down the hill into the creek-bottom, and then scurried off townward. A sentinel down near the stables had caught sight of them, but they were out of view long before his shouts had summoned the corporal of the guard.

No time was to be lost. They were malefactors and vagabonds of the worst character. Two of their number had escaped before and had made it their boast that they could break away from the Russell guard at any time. Directing the sergeant to return to his guard, and hurriedly scribbling a note to the officer of the day, who had his whole troop with him in the saddle out on the prairie, and sending it by the hand of the sergeant-major, the adjutant hurried to his own quarters and called for Van. The news had reached there already. News of any kind travels like wildfire in a garrison, and Van was saddled and bridled before the adjutant reached the gate.

"Bring me my revolver and belt,—quick," he said to the servant, as he swung into saddle. The man darted into the house and came back with the belt and holster.

"I was cleaning your 'Colt,' sir," he said, "but here's the Smith & Wesson," handing up the burnished nickel-plated weapon then in use experimentally on the frontier. Looking only to see that fresh cartridges were in each chamber and that the hammer was on the safety-notch, the adjutant thrust it into the holster, and in an instant he and Van flew through the east gate in rapid pursuit.

Oh, how gloriously Van ran that day! Out on the

prairie the gay guidons of the troops were fluttering in the brilliant sunshine; here, there, everywhere, the skirmish-lines and reserves were dotting the plain ; the air was ringing with the merry trumpet-calls and the stirring words of command. Yet men forgot their drill and reined up on the line to watch Van as he flashed by, wondering, too, what could take the adjutant off at such an hour and at such a pace.

"What's the row?" shouted the commanding officer of one company.

"Prisoners loose," was the answer shouted back, but only indistinctly heard. On went Van like one inspired, and as we cleared the drill-ground and got well out on the open plain in long sweeping curve, we changed our course, aiming more to the right, so as to strike the valley west of the town. It was possible to get there first and head them off. Then suddenly I became aware of something jolting up and down behind me. My hand went back in search : there was no time to look : the prairie just here was cut up with little gopher-holes and criss-crossed by tiny canals from the main *acequia*, or irrigating ditch. It was that wretched Smith & Wesson bobbing up and down in the holster. The Colt revolver of the day was a trifle longer, and my man in changing pistols had not thought to change holsters. This one, made for the Colt, was too long and loose by half an inch, and the pistol was pounding up and down with every stride. Just ahead of us came the flash of the sparkling water in one of the little ditches. Van cleared it in his stride with no effort whatever. Then, just beyond,—oh, fatal trick !—seemingly when in mid-air he changed step, striking the ground with a sudden shock that jarred us both and flung the downward-pointed pistol up against the closely-buttoned holster-flap. There was a sharp report, and my heart stood still an instant. I knew—oh, well I knew it was the death-note of my gallant pet. On he went, never swaying, never swerving, never slackening his racing speed; but, turning in the saddle and glancing back, I saw, just back of the cantle, just to the right of the spine in the glossy brown back, that one tiny, grimy, powder-stained hole. I knew the deadly bullet had ranged downward through his very vitals. I knew that Van had run his last race, was even now rushing towards a goal he would never reach. Fast as he might fly, he could not leave Death behind.

The chase was over. Looking back, I could see the troopers already hastening in pursuit, but we were out of the race. Gently, firmly I drew the rein. Both hands were needed, for Van had never stopped here, and some strange power urged him on now. Full three hundred yards he ran before he would consent to halt. Then I sprang from the saddle and ran to his head. His eyes met mine. Soft and brown, and larger than ever, they gazed imploringly. Pain and bewilderment, strange, wistful pleading, but all the old love and trust, were there as I threw my arms about his neck and bowed his head upon my breast. I could not bear to meet his eyes. I could not look into them and read there the deadly pain and faintness that were rapidly robbing them of their lustre, but that could not shake their faith in his friend and master. No wonder mine grew sightless as his own through swimming tears. I who had killed him could not face his last conscious gaze.

One moment more, and, swaying, tottering first from side to side, poor Van fell with heavy thud upon the turf. Kneeling, I took his head in my arms and strove to call back one sign of recognition; but all that was gone. Van's spirit was ebbing away in some fierce, wild dream: his glazing eyes were fixed on vacancy; his breath came in quick, convulsive gasps; great tremors shook his frame, growing every instant more violent. Suddenly a fiery light shot into his dying eyes. The old high mettle leaped to vivid life, and then, as though the flag had dropped, the starting-drum had tapped, Van's fleeting spirit whirled into his dying race. Lying on his side, his hoofs flew through the air, his powerful limbs worked back and forth swifter than ever in their swiftest gallop, his eyes were aflame, his nostrils wide distended, his chest heaving, and his magnificent machinery running like lightning. Only for a minute, though,—only for one short, painful minute. It was only a half-mile dash,—poor old fellow!—only a hopeless struggle against a rival that never knew defeat. Suddenly all ceased as suddenly as all began. One stiffening quiver, one long sigh, and my pet and pride was gone. Old friends were near him even then. "I was with him when he won his first race at Tucson," said old Sergeant Donnelly, who had ridden to our aid, "and I knowed then he would die racing."

THE END.

WORKS OF FICTION, SELECTED FROM THE CATALOGUE OF J. B. LIPPINCOTT COMPANY, 715–717 MARKET ST., PHILA.

MRS. LEITH ADAMS (MRS. LAFFAN).

12mo, half cloth, 50 cents. Paper cover, 25 cents.

Madelon Lemoine.   **Aunt Hepsy's Foundling.**
Geoffrey Stirling.

"Mrs. Adams's stories are among the best works of fiction. There is a great deal of graphic description, with incident, and fine portraiture of character. We commend them as good specimens of pure and high-toned romance, well worth the reading."—*Phila. Evening Bulletin.*

F. ANSTEY.

A Fallen Idol. 16mo, half cloth, 50 cents. Paper, 25 cents.

"Mr. Anstey's new story will delight the multitudinous public that laughed over 'Vice Versa.' . . . The boy who brings the accursed image to Campion's house, Mr. Bales, the artist's factotum, and, above all, Mr. Yarker, the ex-butler who has turned policeman, are figures whom it is as pleasant to meet as it is impossible to forget."—*London Times.*

WILLIAM ARMSTRONG.

Thekla. A Story of Viennese Musical Life. 12mo, cloth, $1.00.

"The story of Thekla is one of simple beauty. It deals with the life of a young girl, who rejoices in the possession of a glorious voice, and with it earns her livelihood and many warm friends. There are several very masterly bits of work in the book."—*Baltimore American.*

JOSEPHINE W. BATES.

A Blind Lead. The Story of a Mine. 12mo, extra cloth, $1.25.

A Nameless Wrestler. Square 12mo, cloth, $1.00. Paper, 50 cents.

"It is certainly a powerful book. We took up 'A Blind Lead' indifferently enough, but we had read a few pages only before we found it was no ordinary work by no ordinary writer. There are no dull pages, and the interest is continuous from the first chapter to the last."—*Boston Advertiser.*

RHODA BROUGHTON.

Doctor Cupid. 16mo, half cloth, 50 cents. Paper, 25 cents.

"It is a pretty story, sweet in sentiment, and full of delicacy in the telling. The character drawing is excellent; the two girls, Prue and Peggy, deserving high praise as two strong and highly-finished studies."—*Boston Gazette.*

BULWER NOVELS.

Library Edition. 47 volumes. 12mo, cloth, $58.75.
Lord Lytton Edition. 25 volumes. 12mo, per set, cloth, $31.25.

FRANCES HODGSON BURNETT.

Miss Defarge. (No. 1 of *American Novels.*) Square 12mo, cloth, $1.00. Paper, 50 cents.

"A good book to be put in the satchel for a railway trip or ocean voyage."—*Chicago Current.*

"Mrs. Burnett's stories are always bright and interesting."—*Baltimore American.*

MRS. H. LOVETT CAMERON.

16mo, half cloth, 50 cents. Paper, 25 cents.

In a Grass Country: A Story of Love and Sport.
Vera Neville.   Pure Gold.
A Life's Mistake.   Worth Winning.
This Wicked World.   A Devout Lover.
A Lost Wife.   The Cost of a Lie.

"Mrs. Cameron's numerous efforts in the line of fiction have won for her a wide circle of admirers. Her experience in novel writing, as well as her skill in inventing and delineating characters, enables her to put before the reading public stories that are full of interest and pure in tone."—*Harrisburg Telegraph.*

ROSA N. CAREY.

Stories for Girls. 12mo, cloth, illustrated, $1.25 per volume. Complete set in box, $3.75.

Esther.   Aunt Diana.
Merle's Crusade.

PUBLICATIONS OF J. B. LIPPINCOTT COMPANY.

ROSA N. CAREY (continued).

Novels. 16mo, half cloth, 50 cents. Paper, 25 cents.

Wooed and Married.
Nellie's Memories.
Queenie's Whim.
Not Like Other Girls.
Wee Wifie.

Barbara Heathcote's Trial.
For Lilias.
Robert Ord's Atonement.
Uncle Max.
Only the Governess.

"Mrs. Carey's novels may be compared to a tranquil backwater out of the main current of the turbid stream of modern fiction. The graces and charities of domestic life are treated by her with never-failing sympathy and refinement."—*London Athenæum.*

G. I. CERVUS.

White Feathers. 12mo, cloth, $1.00.
A Model Wife. 12mo, cloth, $1.00.
Cut: A Story of West Point. 12mo, cloth, $1.00. Paper, 50 cents.

"Mr. Cerves is a keen analyst of character and a vigorous writer. His books are always welcome and thoroughly readable."—*Boston Literary World.*

GRAHAM CLAYTOR.

Pleasant Waters. 12mo, cloth, $1.00.
Wheat and Tares. 12mo, cloth, $1.25.

"Very readable indeed. We laid the book down with the feeling that the author had done his work well. We haven't books enough on the Southern people. The vein has been worked but the mine has not been thoroughly developed. The author has ploughed in this field and turned up some good furrows."—*New York Herald.*

MRS. B. S. CUNNINGHAM.

For Honor's Sake. 12mo, cloth, $1.50.
In Sancho Panza's Pit. 12mo, cloth, $1.50.

"Mrs. Cunningham's style is pleasing and her stories attractive."—*Utica Herald.*

"'Sancho Panza's Pit' is a novel of unusual power and artistic merit."—*New York Home Journal.*

HERBERT G. DICK.

Mistaken Paths. 12mo, cloth, $1.25.

"The story is well developed and the moral sound. The characters are in no way overdrawn, and the interest often intense."—*American Bookseller*.

GEORGE THOMAS DOWLING.

The Wreckers. A Social Study. 12mo, cloth, $1.25.

"A book like 'The Wreckers' will help better to a comprehension of our duties to each other and a proper understanding of the rights and needs of labor than would volume upon volume of essays on political and social economy."—*Philadelphia Record*.

GEORGE ELIOT.

Complete Works. 24 volumes. 16mo, cloth, $42.00.
8 volumes. 12mo, cloth, $8.00.

EDGAR FAWCETT.

A Demoralizing Marriage. (No. 4 of *American Novel Series*.) Square 12mo, cloth, $1.00. Paper, 50 cents.

Douglas Duane, and "Sinfire," by Julian Hawthorne. (No. 3 of *American Novel Series*.) Square 12mo, cloth, $1.00. Paper, 50 cents.

"Mr. Fawcett is one of the few really good American novelists, and his grace of language is not eclipsed by any other writer in the country."—*Harrisburg Telegraph*.

MRS. FORRESTER.

16mo, half cloth, 50 cents. Paper cover, 25 cents.

Dolores.   Roy and Viola.
Diana Carew.   My Lord and My Lady.
Mignon.   I Have Lived and Loved.
Viva.   June.
Rhona.   Once Again.

"Mrs. Forrester is always good in sentiment and description, and her stories are excellent reading."—*Saturday Evening Post*.

EDWARD J. GOODMAN.

Too Curious. 16mo, half cloth, 50 cents. Paper 25 cents.

"The author of 'Too Curious' has done a real service both to readers and writers by proving that even now a novel can be produced which is at once artistic, thrilling, and original."—*London Tablet*.

www.ingramcontent.com/pod-product-compliance
Lightning Source LLC
Chambersburg PA
CBHW032147230426
43672CB00011B/2476